Vincent Price
COOKING PRICE-WISE

A Culinary Legacy

Preface by Victoria Price

Foreword by V.B. Price

Vincent Price

DOVER PUBLICATIONS, INC.
Mineola, New York

Bibliographical Note

This Dover edition, first published in 2017, is an unabridged republication of the work originally published by Transworld Publishers Ltd., London, in 1971. The original book was based on the Thames Television series with Vincent Price, produced by Charmian Watford and Bob Murray for I.D. Television Ltd. A Table of Equivalents has been provided for some ingredients in the original recipes. A new Preface by Victoria Price and a new Foreword by V.B. Price have been included in this edition. The excerpts from Vincent Price's journals are reproduced with minor corrections. Peter Fuller has kindly provided the journal material for this edition.

International Standard Book Number

ISBN-13: 978-0-486-81907-5
ISBN-10: 0-486-81907-8

Manufactured in the United States by LSC Communications
81907801   2017
www.doverpublications.com

Contents

page

Preface to the New Edition
by Victoria Price   v

Foreword to the New Edition
by V.B. Price   vii

Original Introduction by Vincent Price   xiii

Section One . . . Potato Recipes   1

Section Two . . . Meat Recipes   27

Section Three . . . Bacon Recipes   55

Section Four . . . Rice Recipes   77

Section Five . . . Cream, Milk, and Yogurt Recipes   111

Section Six

    Part One . . . Cheese Recipes   143

    Part Two . . . Coffee   166

The Culinary Legacy of the Price Family   173

    The Beginning of the Price Family
    Culinary Legacy   174

    Vincent's Culinary Journey Begins   178

    The Culinary Legacy Continues . . .   185

Table of Equivalents   188

Index to Recipes   189

Preface to the New Edition

In 1971, my father was asked to host *Cooking Price-Wise*, a British television show on cooking—or cookery, as the English call it. He eagerly agreed.

First of all, he was an Anglophile. So, anything that gave him an excuse to be or work in England always earned his immediate Yes. Second, in the United States he had become almost as well known as a gourmet chef as he was as an actor. Now he was eager to share his love and advocacy of the culinary arts with the British public. But mostly, third, he loved the premise of the show, because it matched his life philosophy: Anyone can see and taste the world without ever having to leave their hometown. All the ingredients for both an extraordinary life and an extraordinary meal must first be discovered within our own imaginations.

The show, however, proved to be short-lived; it is even hard to find copies of it on video. I was thrilled to finally see some clips of it a few years ago. It did *not* turn out to be what I had expected. The program was filmed on rather a low budget, and, as a result, hilarity often ensued. But, as we learned from the inimitable Julia Child, hilarity often ensues in the kitchen. Moreover, hilarity is far better than the alternative. Because, let's face it, all culinary endeavors have a margin for error. And laughing at our mistakes is a far better way of learning to be a better cook than having a hissy fit. My father always laughed and learned from his mistakes. So, at one point, when his tiny television show kitchen left him no empty surfaces on which to put down the turkey he had just trussed, while he tried and failed to open the oven door, he just nonchalantly put the turkey on the floor, chuckled . . . and went on with the show. His dear friend Julia would have thoroughly approved.

Although the show did not have a long run, this cookbook has become a collector's item. So, I was very grateful for this opportunity to republish it. Furthermore, this new edition has allowed us to share even more of my father's lifelong adventure with food and fine dining—as well as the Price family's culinary legacy. We have been able to include some of the recipes from my great-grandfather's cookbook, as well as sections of my father's journal from his first trip to Europe, taken when he was seventeen years old! I've even tossed in a few of our favorite family recipes as I remember them.

Lastly, I am particularly grateful to be able to include a short essay about my father that was written in 2011 to honor what would have been his 100th birthday. Never published, this insightful piece by my brother, V.B. Price, allows a glimpse of my father that is deeply meaningful and illuminating.

Cooking Price-Wise, as it all turns out, was far more than a cookbook or cookery show. It is a way of life. *Cooking Price-Wise* means seeing the world as your oyster, and then learning how to enjoy it by sharing it with others. My father always believed that a man who limits his interests limits his life. His interest in cooking came first and foremost from his love of food—shopping for it, preparing it, eating it, but mostly savoring it with others in gratitude and celebration. He would be absolutely delighted to know that he still gets to do all of that with all of you.

So, without further ado, dig in and enjoy.

As he always wrote when he autographed one of his cookbooks— Bon Appétit!

VICTORIA PRICE
2017

Foreword to the New Edition

Vincent Price:
A Legacy of Pleasure

It almost goes without saying, that Vincent Price was many things to many people—more than most, I'd say. He was a man possessed of a joyous curiosity, and it took him wherever he wanted to go. His hunger for knowledge was utterly genuine. It allowed him to do his work with the ease and precision of a master and a pro. He was, as everyone knows, a marvelous actor, an arch comedian, an educator and lecturer, a lover and student of the arts, a writer of insightful and moving books, a creative philanthropist, a tireless champion of other people's talent, and, above all, a master appreciator. He really was all those things even if he didn't think of himself in that way. And that's why he could also be such a good father and such a fine friend. He was grateful for his fame, but never believed it. He saw himself as a student devoted to the practice of learning and refining his talents. That's how I knew him.

He used to say that there was no excuse in this world to ever be bored. And I don't think he ever was. He loved being alive, though I don't think he would have called himself a happy person. He was too self-critical for that. He wanted the best out of himself, and he, like all of us, often found that hard to come by.

But he would be the first to say that his life was full of amazing good luck, that he was—what he said of me because of my wonderful marriage—Fortune's Child. He'd never boast that he made the best of it, but he did. That was the hallmark of his life as an artist and a scholar—he made the most of what came along, and he always felt that the right doors opened at the right time for him and that opportunity appeared just when he needed it. His expression for that sensation of Lady Luck smiling upon him was "I've fallen into a tub of butter."

It's the depth and delight of his love of life, of living each day all out, of trying to never miss an experience or take anything for granted, that was the great gift he gave to his friends and children. Wherever he went, people loved to be around him. His enthusiasm and attentiveness made us all feel empowered.

His legacy, from my perspective, is a philosophy and a way of life. I'm sure he would have demurred at the idea that he could serve as a model of how to live a full, rich life, no matter how star-crossed, self-critical, or anxiety-ridden one might be. But at seventy-one years old, and after nearly twenty years since his death, that's how he seems to me now. He was a man full of romantic enthusiasms who didn't, as it turns out, marry well. Domestic sufferings seriously wounded him. He was what could be called a workaholic, driven to maximize his talent and keep his enterprises flourishing despite many setbacks, and while escaping many insoluble dilemmas and shortcomings. He suffered from feelings of inadequacy. He enjoyed good health, but had numerous physical difficulties. He had all the troubles and despairs that most of us do. And he reproached himself with vigor and consistency.

Yet he was an exuberant, unstoppable person, animated by native joy and enthusiasm that simply could not be diluted for long by pressure or disappointment. He knew what the great consolations of life really are—curiosity, generosity, gratitude, and appreciation. He knew that life rewards those who love it. He knew that the laws of energy eventually made good on the effort one expends to do one's best, even if making good often comes about in completely unexpected ways. He valued talent and humor with equal intensity. And he had a genius for having fun, which rubbed off on everyone who was with him.

During his last days, when he was in his eighties, struggling with emphysema, Parkinson's disease, and a failing heart, even then his joy gave him endurance. Whether recounting from memory the provenance of works of art from his own seemingly endless collections, to savoring the making of a fine risotto, to getting sweetly silly at word games, entertaining and cheering up old friends, or raptly watching the news with as much fascination as he gave his orchids, Dad remained true to who he had been all his life, an embodiment of the pleasure principle, giving those around him as much pleasure with as little pain as it was possible for him to share.

V.B. PRICE
2011

Vincent Price
COOKING
PRICE-WISE

A Culinary Legacy

– Original Edition –

A host of exotic recipes—things to eat and drink from all over the world—and each one made from ingredients easily available from your local shops or supermarket . . .

Introduction

Hello, I'm Vincent Price. There are three things that really turn me on, as the current saying goes, one is work—I'm never really happy when I'm not working—another is art, and the third is food.

This book is the follow-up to a television series I made recently, which was all about food. I didn't invent the recipes in this book, or in the series. I collected them.

One of the nice things about travelling is finding out what people eat, and how they serve their food, both in the grand restaurants and in the small inns and homes of the people.

As an actor I get more chance than most people of travelling, and I seem to be constantly collecting new recipes, which is fine, because when I do get home I try them out.

You may ask why they asked me—Vincent Price, star of countless horror movies—to be a TV chef.

Well, let me assure you it's by no means my first foray into the world of gastronomy. I've already written several books on the subject—including *A Treasury of Great Recipes, A National Treasury of Cookery,* and *Come into the Kitchen Cook Book* in collaboration with my wife, Mary.

And I'd like to take up that point about the horror movies, too. You see I started in films back in 1938 with a film called 'Service de Luxe' in which I was Constance Bennett's leading man, but it wasn't until 1953, with a film called—you remember—'House of Wax'—that I first got involved in horror movies.

Or look at it another way. I've made over eighty films and only about twenty of them could be described as horror films. The reason, I suppose, that I've got stuck with the label of 'horror king' is that I'm so good at playing that kind of role.

I've also been called 'one of America's leading authorities on fine art'. I didn't say it, but it's true all the same. I do have a large art collection of my own. I act as buyer for Sears Roebuck as well.

Which naturally brings me back to cookery. People always seem afraid of food from other countries—they'll eat spaghetti, for instance, if it comes out of a tin, chopped up short and smothered in tomato sauce, but the real thing, no matter how available it is, is quite beyond them.

Then, of course, you get the folks who think that foreign food is full of things that you can only get on special order from Harrods, and I must admit that the way some cookery books are written, you'd think that was so.

So I was glad to accept the challenge when the producers of the series 'Cooking Price-Wise' asked me to do the shows. Their one condition was that all the ingredients in all the recipes must be readily available in just about any group of food shops or supermarket.

We spent hours arguing as to whether a particular item could be found in the local shops—in fact, one of the producers even rang up a Bolton supermarket to ask them whether they stocked tins of bean-shoots. They did, so you'll find them in one of the recipes. We also found that soy sauce was obtainable in Oban, in Scotland.

In researching the programmes we found out some pretty extraordinary facts—like that the British eat some 198 pounds of potatoes, per person, per year. That most of the rice eaten in Europe is imported from America. That 30 per cent of the British never buy cream. That bacon was brought to Britain by the Romans, and so on, and so on.

The programmes were arranged so that each programme contained recipes built around one central ingredient, so that is how we've arranged the chapters in this book.

One of the great things about collecting, is that what you collect usually has a story behind it. This is true of art, of coins, antiques, medals, stamps, cigarette cards or whatever. It's certainly true of recipes. Some of these stories we've put in the book because it makes the dish just that little bit more interesting if you know the story behind it

I must warn you, though, that some of the recipes come from a rather far-away place called Britain! Now the people of this country have very strange eating habits. Instead of washing their hands very thoroughly and eating with their clean fingers they use what they call 'Knives and Forks'—which they get from a drawer, where they've all been lying collecting dust for anything up to several days since being washed—these implements are not washed again before they're used!

However, I can assure the more squeamish among you that I have only chosen the cleanest recipes from this unfortunate land.

So with your cooker, instead of a jet-plane, come with me on a gastronomic tour of the world . . .

VINCENT PRICE
1971

SECTION ONE
Potato Recipes

It may seem strange to start with the common spud—what could be more English—in a book full of international recipes?

Well, let me set you right. The potato comes from Peru, and was brought to Europe by the Conquistadores, who came from Spain, in the early fifteenth century.

To the Incas the potato was almost a sacred object. It was grown in potato patches fertilized with human blood, and it figured prominently in their rituals.

It was Raleigh, or was it Drake, or, as some scribes have it, Hawkins, who brought the potato to Britain in 1578. Anyhow, whoever it was, the British have been eating it with practically everything ever since.

Contrary to most housewives' menus—which tend to dismiss the potato with a wave of the masher or the chipping knife, the potato is a very versatile item. I think you'll agree when you've tried some of the dishes I've selected for you.

It really is international too. Take the first dish. The recipe comes from Savoie, and the dish is called 'Pommes de terre Savoyarde'. It's a delicious combination of cream, and cheese, and potatoes. That part of the world, high on the French-Italian border, is famous for its dairy produce, and this simple, inexpensive dish is one of the nicest things to come out of that region.

1

POMMES DE TERRE SAVOYARDE

Potatoes in Cream au Gratin

Serves 4

- ✦ *Potatoes*
- ✦ *Light cream*
- ✦ *Butter*
- ✦ *Salt*
- ✦ *Pepper*
- ✦ *Cheese*
- ✦ *Garlic* (*optional*)

Slice 8 medium potatoes very thinly. Put into a saucepan with salted boiling water to cover. Bring to the boil and boil for 3 minutes. Drain.

Rub garlic clove around buttered oval baking-dish, about 12 in. long, put a layer of half the potatoes. Sprinkle with ½ teaspoon salt and freshly ground pepper. Sprinkle with 4 oz. grated cheese, and cover with remaining potatoes.

Add 1 pint of light cream and sprinkle with 4 oz. grated cheese. Bring to the boil, over directed heat and simmer for 15 minutes. Put under grill for 2 or 3 minutes or until browned.

Potatoes, because they're found in just about every country, can cross frontiers recipe-wise. Take the vichyssoise, or chilled potato soup. I suppose it is French in origin because of the name, but, of course, it is found all over Europe.

In New York, they have a variation of this recipe which they call Manhattan Vichyssoise, the trick here is the addition of carrots. This gives the basic soup a delicious originality.

MANHATTAN VICHYSSOISE

Serves 4–6

+ *Potatoes*
+ *Carrots*
+ *Leek*
+ *Chicken stock*
+ *Salt*
+ *Pepper*
+ *Cream*

Soup:

Into a saucepan put 12 oz. peeled, diced potatoes, 6 oz. sliced carrots, 1 leek, sliced (white part only), and 1½ pints of chicken stock. Bring to the boil and simmer for 25 minutes, or until vegetables are tender.

In an electric blender pureé half the vegetables and liquid at a time of 30 seconds on high speed. Empty into mixing-bowl.

Stir in a pinch of white pepper, 1 teaspoon salt and ½ pint of cream.

Presentation:

Serve in chilled bowls, icy cold, with a topping of shredded raw carrot.

Holland, as you all know, is famous for its sea-walls, or 'dikes'. As land is reclaimed from the sea, massive earthwork walls are set up to keep out the water.

Well, I know a Dutch recipe which celebrates the construction of these walls in a unique way. In this dish, which is called Fish Fillets Noord Zee, creamed potatoes are used to represent the dikes, while the sea is represented by fish in sort-of lakes, made by the potato walls.

I think the important thing here is that it shows how important the method of presentation is to a meal. Fish and mash needn't always be a spoonful of mashed potato on one side of a plate and the fish piled up on the other. A little imagination, and you can create all sorts of dishes of your own—just by the design of the food arranged on the platter.

Another thing to be learnt from the preparation of this dish is the importance of using the juices the food was originally cooked in, to make the sauce. This way, you give the sauce a really good flavour.

If you don't feel like cooking fish, however, other foods can be placed between the potato walls—for instance, you can serve all your vegetables beautifully arranged on one large dish, or, a mixture of meat and vegetables can be divided by the walls. Anyhow, the important thing is to use your imagination!

FISH FILLETS NOORD ZEE

Serves 4

- ✦ *Potatoes*
- ✦ *Butter*
- ✦ *Cream*
- ✦ *Salt*
- ✦ *White pepper*
- ✦ *Fillets of plaice*
- ✦ *Dry white wine*
- ✦ *Lemons*
- ✦ *Mushrooms*
- ✦ *Shrimps*
- ✦ *Scallops*
- ✦ *Herring roes*
- ✦ *Eggs*
- ✦ *Flour*
- ✦ *Parsley*

Cook 4 medium potatoes in salted water until very tender. Drain and mash. Beat in 3 tablespoons butter and enough hot cream to make fluffy potatoes that are still stiff enough to be pressed through a fluted pastry tube. Season to taste with salt and white pepper. Keep warm over simmering water.

Poach 4 fillets of plaice (about 1¼ lb.) in a cup of water with ½ pint of dry white wine, the juice of 1 lemon, ½ teaspoon salt and ¼ teaspoon white pepper for 5 minutes. Remove fillets and keep warm. Boil liquid over high heat until reduced to ¼ pint.

Heat 1 tablespoon butter in each of 4 small frying-pans. In one sauté 4 oz. button mushrooms for 5 minutes. In another, 4 oz. shrimps for 5 minutes. In a third, toss 4 oz. herring roes floured for 5 minutes; in the last, cook 4 sliced scallops for 5 minutes.

Fill a forcing bag, fitted with a large fluted tube, with the mashed potatoes and press out a fluted ribbon down the centre of a large serving-platter. On one side press out 3 ribbons from centre to edge of platter, making 4 evenly divided compartments. Arrange the fillets on the other side in the long compartment. Put platter into a warm oven to keep warm.

Sauce:

In saucepan beat 2 eggs with 1 tablespoon flour and ½ pint cream. Strain ¼ pint of reduced fish liquid into the egg-cream mixture and cook, stirring rapidly until sauce is hot and slightly thickened. Be careful not to let it boil. Stir in ¼ teaspoon salt, or to taste, and 1 tablespoon lemon juice.

Presentation:

Pour sauce over the fish fillets only and garnish with parsley.

I've always been told that the Scots were a miserly race of people. This may be so, or it may be false. What I can positively state is that they've never come up with a dish which was dedicated solely to misers. That privilege is reserved for the Welsh.

I found this recipe in Carmarthenshire, and the Welsh name is Feest y Cybydd, or Miser's Feast.

Apparently, this dish was very popular in that part of the principality about one hundred years ago. The miser was supposed to eat the potatoes mashed up in the liquid one day. He would then keep the slices of bacon to be eaten the following day with plain boiled potatoes.

FEEST Y CYBYDD

Serves 4
Cooking time: 1 hour

+ *1½ lb. potatoes, peeled thinly*
+ *2 large onions, peeled and sliced*
+ *1 pint stock or water*
+ *8–12 oz. sliced bacon or ham*
+ *Parsley, chopped*

Place potatoes in saucepan or casserole. Add onions and a little salt. Cover with stock and bring to the boil. Place bacon on top of potatoes and onions. Replace lid, simmer until potatoes are cooked (about 1 hour—most of the water will then be absorbed). Sprinkle with chopped parsley.

COQUILLES ST. JACQUES

+ *5 scallops*
+ *A little butter*
+ *Fine white breadcrumbs*
+ *Salt and pepper*
+ *Duchesse potatoes*

Ask the fishmonger to clean the scallops and keep them in the half-shell. Place them on a baking-dish with a generous lump of butter on each one. Bake in a fairly hot oven 400° F. or Gas Mark 6 for approximately 30 minutes depending on the size of the scallops, basting them frequently with the butter and liquor which will come out of the scallops. When the scallops are tender (test the thick white part with a fork) make a ring of Duchesse potatoes around the edge of each shell. Sprinkle the top of each scallop with fine breadcrumbs and add a dot of butter on each. Season and place under a very hot grill until browned.

N.B. For Duchesse potatoes, add 1 beaten egg and 1 oz. butter to 1 lb. mashed potatoes. Put into forcing bag with star nozzle for piping.

CROQUETTES

Serves 4
Cooking time 3–4 minutes

+ *1 lb. potatoes prepared as Duchesse Mixture*
+ *1 oz. flour*
+ *1 egg (beaten)*
+ *2 oz. breadcrumbs*
+ *Prepare Duchesse Mix by mixing beaten egg and 1 oz. butter with potatoes*

Divide the mixture and with floured hands roll into corks or balls. Brush with beaten egg and coat with breadcrumbs. Fry in deep fat until golden brown. Drain on absorbent paper. Serve hot as an accompaniment to meat, fish or savoury dishes.

Variations:
Following can be added to mixture:
1. *Parsley*
2. *Grated nutmeg*
3. *Cooked diced onions*
4. *Chopped hard-boiled eggs*
5. *Chopped shrimps or prawns*

FARMHOUSE CHICKEN CASSEROLE

Serves 4
Cooking time: 1 hour at 375° F. (Gas Mark 5)

+ *4 chicken joints*
+ *2 oz. cornflour (or flour)*
+ *1 lb. potatoes, peeled and quartered*
+ *4 rashers of bacon streaky, derinded and diced*
+ *2 oz. mushrooms, quartered*
+ *6 spring onions*
+ *¾ pint chicken stock*

Toss chicken joints in seasoned cornflour, fry until golden brown. Place in a casserole with the potatoes. Fry bacon, mushrooms, and onions until golden and add to the casserole. Add stock to the fry-pan, and stir until boiling. Pour into the casserole and cover, bake for 1 hour or until tender. Sprinkle with chopped spring onions or chives, add salt and pepper if necessary.

SHROPSHIRE FIDGET PIE

Serves 4
Cooking time: 1¼–1½ hours at 400° F (Gas Mark 6)

+ *1 lb. potatoes, peeled and sliced ⅛ in. thick*
+ *8 oz. apples, peeled, cored and sliced*
+ *8 oz. streaky bacon, derinded, cut in small pieces*
+ *1 tablespoon demerara sugar*
+ *¼ pint stock or water*
+ *8 oz. potato pastry or shortcrust pastry*

Place potatoes, apples and bacon in a greased pie-dish. Sprinkle with sugar, salt and pepper; add stock. Roll out pastry and place over pie filling (use pie funnel). Bake for 1¼–1½ hours.

PARMENTIER SOUP

+ 1 *lb. potatoes*
+ 2–3 *leeks (white part only)*
+ 2 *oz. butter*
+ 1 *pint stock or water*
+ *½ gill* [2 *oz.*] *milk*
+ *½ gill* [2 *oz.*] *cream*
+ *Salt and pepper*
+ *Chopped parsley, chives or chervil*

Peel the potatoes thinly, and cut into thick slices. Clean the leeks, cut into pieces, and sauté in half the butter, taking care not to brown them. Add potatoes, stock and salt. Cook until the vegetables are soft. Rub through a sieve, or put into a liquidizer. Return to the saucepan, adjust the seasoning, and re-heat. Just before serving, stir in the rest of the butter, milk, and cream. Sprinkle with freshly chopped parsley and serve hot or cold.

SAURE KARTOFFELN

*This is a German dish—the name means
'Sour Potatoes'*

Serves 4
Cooking time: 30 minutes

- ✦ 1½ *lb. potatoes, peeled*
- ✦ 4 *oz. lean bacon, derinded and cut into small pieces*
- ✦ 1 *oz. plain flour*
- ✦ ½ *pint stock*
- ✦ 1 *tablespoon wine vinegar*
- ✦ 1 *teaspoon sugar*
- ✦ 8 *oz. French beans, sliced (or 1 packet frozen)*

Boil potatoes until just cooked, cut into slices about ¼ in. thick. Fry bacon gently in butter. Add the flour and cook gently without browning; add the stock gradually and allow to boil. Add the potatoes, salt, pepper, vinegar, sugar and French beans. Simmer for 30 minutes.

CREOLE POTATO SALAD

- ✦ 1 *lb. cooked potatoes*
- ✦ 1 *tablespoon grated onion*
- ✦ ½ *pint shrimps or prawns*
- ✦ 1 *hard-boiled egg, sliced*
- ✦ ¼ *pint mayonnaise*
- ✦ 1 *tablespoon tomato sauce*
- ✦ *Little chopped parsley*

After boiling the potatoes in salted water, drain, remove the skins and cut potatoes into dice. Add mayonnaise. Mix ingredients together while potatoes are still warm. Add chopped parsley.

POTATO POLONY

Serves 4
Cooking time: 50–60 minutes at 400° F. (Gas Mark 6)

+ 1 *lb. potatoes, peeled and boiled*
+ 1 *lb. sausagemeat*
+ 1 *small onion, peeled and finely chopped*
+ 1 *teaspoon Worcester sauce*
+ ½ *teaspoon mixed herbs*
+ 1 *egg, beaten*
+ 2 *eggs, hard-boiled*
+ 3 *tablespoons white breadcrumbs*
+ 1½ *oz. bacon fat or dripping*

Prepare vegetables and eggs. Mash potato with sausagemeat, onion, Worcester sauce, mixed herbs and half the beaten egg. Shape into a roll: make a hollow down the centre. Place the hard-boiled eggs along the hollow and close over. Brush the roll all over with the remaining beaten egg, coat with breadcrumbs and place in hot fat in a baking-tin. Baste with fat and bake for approx. 50–60 minutes.

Serve hot or cold.

PAN CREOLE POTATOES (CANADA)

Serves 4–6

+ 1½ lb. potatoes
+ 2 medium-sized onions
+ 1 good tablespoon fat
+ Salt and pepper
+ 3 tablespoons tomato ketchup

Peel the potatoes thinly, and cut into slices ⅛ in. thick. Melt the fat in a frying-pan, add the potatoes and onion. Cover and cook over a low heat until tender (about 35 minutes). Turn several times during cooking. Combine salt, pepper and the ketchup and spread over the potatoes. Cover and cook for a further 10 minutes, turning the mixture again.

POMMES DAUPHINOISE (FRANCE)

Serves 4
Oven temperature: 375° F. (Gas Mark 5)

+ 1 lb. potatoes
+ 1 egg
+ ½ pint milk
+ 4 oz. grated cheese
+ 2 oz. butter
+ Salt and pepper
+ Grated nutmeg
+ Clove of garlic

Peel the potatoes thinly and cut into slices ⅛ in. thick. Rub the clove of garlic around a fireproof dish and butter it well, then put the potatoes into the dish. Season well with the salt and pepper, and grated nutmeg. Beat up the egg in the milk adding 2 oz. cheese to it, then pour over the potatoes. Sprinkle with the other 2 oz. cheese, adding the butter in small pieces, over the surface and bake in the oven for about an hour—until the top is nicely browned.

POTATOES WITH SOUR CREAM (POLAND)

Serves 4

- ✦ 1 *lb. potatoes*
- ✦ 2 *tablespoons butter*
- ✦ *Salt and pepper*
- ✦ 1 *tablespoon chives*
- ✦ 5 *oz. carton of sour cream*

Peel the potatoes thinly, and cook in salted water till just under-cooked. Drain and cut the potatoes into dice. Melt the butter in a frying-pan, brown the potatoes in the fat and sprinkle with salt and pepper. Add the chives and cream, cover, and allow to simmer over a very low heat till all the cream is absorbed. Serve hot as an accompaniment.

LANCASHIRE HOTPOT

Serves 6
Cooking time: 2½ hours at 325° F. (Gas Mark 3)

+ 1–1½ *lb. potatoes, peeled*
+ 1½ *lb. middle neck of mutton, trimmed*
+ 2 *sheep's kidneys*
+ 2 *large onions, peeled*
+ ½ *pint stock*

Slice potatoes ¼ in. thick, cut mutton and kidney into neat pieces, slice onion. Place layers of the meat and vegetables in a greased casserole, salt and pepper well and finish with a layer of potatoes. Add about ½ pint stock or water and cover with the casserole lid or aluminium foil. Bake for about 2½ hours removing the lid for the last half-hour to brown the potatoes. Add small dabs of dripping or butter if potatoes get too dry during cooking.

Serve with pickled red cabbage or crumbled Lancashire cheese.

LYONNAISE POTATOES

Serves 4

+ 1 *lb. potatoes, peeled and sliced*
+ 1 *onion, peeled and sliced*

Parboil potatoes; this takes about 3–5 minutes. Lightly fry onion rings until pale golden brown. Remove from the pan, then fry potato slices. When cooked, add onions and fry both together until crisp and brown.

MINESTRONE

Serves 8
Cooking time: 1½ hours

- ✦ *4 oz. potatoes, peeled and diced*
- ✦ *2 oz. carrots, peeled and diced*
- ✦ *2 oz. turnips, peeled and diced*
- ✦ *1 medium onion, peeled and diced*
- ✦ *1 stalk celery, washed and chopped*
- ✦ *1 oz. streaky bacon, derinded*
- ✦ *2 tablespoons tomato purée*
- ✦ *2½ pints stock*
- ✦ *2 bayleaves*
- ✦ *1 oz. macaroni*
- ✦ *¼ medium cabbage, shredded*
- ✦ *1 teaspoon sugar*
- ✦ *Parmesan cheese*

Prepare vegetables. Cut bacon into pieces, fry gently in a little butter until soft. Add vegetables and continue frying for 2–3 minutes. Stir in tomato purée and gradually add stock, bayleaves and macaroni. Bring to boil, add salt and pepper, cover and simmer for 1 hour, add shredded cabbage and cook for a further 30 minutes. Remove bayleaves, add sugar and serve accompanied by Parmesan cheese.

POTATO YAHNI (GREECE)

Serves 4–6

+ *2½ lb. potatoes*
+ *1 lb. chopped onions*
+ *1 lb. peeled and chopped tomatoes*
+ *1 tablespoon sugar*
+ *¼ pint olive oil*
+ *Salt and pepper*
+ *Bayleaf (if liked)*

Peel the potatoes thinly and cut into uniform size. Heat the oil and fry the onions until golden brown. Add the tomatoes and simmer until soft with the sugar and bayleaf. Finally add the potatoes, seasoning and enough water to half cover them. Cook until the potatoes are soft and the sauce is thick. This usually is served as a main meal.

MULLIGATAWNY SOUP

Serves 4
Cooking time: 45 minutes

- ✦ 1 *lb. potatoes, peeled and sliced*
- ✦ 1 *large onion, peeled and sliced*
- ✦ 1 *large carrot, peeled and sliced*
- ✦ 1 *cooking apple, peeled and sliced*
- ✦ 2 *oz. butter*
- ✦ 2 *tablespoons curry powder*
- ✦ 2 *teaspoons tomato purée*
- ✦ 2½ *pints beef stock*
- ✦ 1 *lemon, rind and juice*

Prepare vegetables and apple, melt butter and fry together for 2–3 minutes with curry powder and tomato purée. Add stock, salt and pepper, bring to boil, cover and simmer for 45 minutes. Sieve or liquidize, reheat and add lemon juice. Garnish with rind of lemon.

PERUVIAN PEPPERS

Serves 4
Cooking time: 40 minutes at 350° F. (Gas Mark 4)

+ 1 *lb. potatoes, peeled, parboiled and diced*
+ 8 *oz. raw minced beef*
+ 2 *medium onions, peeled and finely chopped*
+ 2 *tablespoons tomato purée*
+ 2 *tomatoes, scalded, skinned and chopped*
+ ½ *pint stock*
+ 1 *bayleaf*
+ 4 *peppers, cored and scalded*

Prepare vegetables and fry potatoes until golden. Brown the mince, add onions and cook till soft. Stir in tomato purée, tomatoes, stock and bayleaf. Simmer for 10 minutes. Remove bayleaf, add potatoes, salt and pepper. Fill peppers with mixture and bake for 30 minutes.

SARDINIAN GNOCCHI (ITALY)

Serves 4

+ 1 *lb. potatoes*
+ 6 *oz. plain flour*
+ 1 *egg*
+ *Salt and pepper*
+ *Pinch of nutmeg*

Tomato Sauce:

+ 1 *streaky rasher of bacon*
+ 1 *large tin peeled tomatoes* (14 *oz. size*)
+ 1 *dessertspoon flour*
+ 1 *large finely chopped onion*
+ 1 *tablespoon butter or oil*
+ *Squeeze of garlic*
+ *Salt and pepper and sugar to taste*
+ *Grated Parmesan cheese*

Peel the potatoes thinly and boil in salted water until tender. Meanwhile, make the sauce—cut the bacon into small pieces and sauté in the butter with the onion. Add the flour and cook for a few seconds without browning. Stir in the tomatoes and season to taste. Allow to cook gently for about 5 minutes and then keep hot. Drain the potatoes, mash well adding the flour, egg, salt, pepper and nutmeg. With floured hands make a 'long roll' about ½ in. thick and cut into slices 1 in. in length. Drop into a pan of boiling salted water and simmer gently for approximately 5 minutes. Drain well, put into a warm serving-dish and pour the tomato sauce over the top. Sprinkle liberally with grated Parmesan cheese.

POTATO AND FISH CHOWDER

Serves 4
Cooking time: about 20 minutes

Chowder is a speciality on the Atlantic coast of America—a soup-stew with infinite variations on the fish, potatoes and onions theme.

+ 1 *large onion, peeled and chopped*
+ 3 *rashers streaky bacon, chopped (derinded)*
+ 1 *lb. potatoes, peeled*
+ 1 *lb. cod or haddock, filleted, skinned and cut up*
+ 4 *oz. mushrooms*
+ ½ *pint stock or water*
+ 2 *tablespoons double cream*
+ *Parsley, chopped*

Fry the bacon and onion without browning, add potatoes (cut into ½ in. dice), fish, mushrooms, stock or water, salt and pepper.

Simmer gently for 15 minutes until fish and potatoes are cooked, cool slightly. Stir in the cream and sprinkle with parsley before serving.

SWEETCORN AND POTATO PIE

Serves 4

Cooking time: 20 minutes at 400° F. (Gas Mark 6)

✦ 1 *lb. mashed potatoes*

✦ 2 *medium onions, peeled and finely chopped*

✦ 1 *clove of garlic, crushed (optional)*

✦ 5 *oz. streaky bacon*

✦ 1 *can creamed sweetcorn*

Fry onions and garlic. Remove rind from bacon. Cut into pieces and reserve a few pieces to make bacon rolls for decoration. Mix together bacon, onion and corn, place in an ovenproof dish, add salt and pepper. Pipe mashed potatoes on top, bake and decorate with grilled bacon rolls.

FILLET OF BEEF ANGUS

Serves 6
Cooking time: 40 minutes at 425° F. (Gas Mark 7)

+ 1 *piece of fillet of beef (approx.* 1½ *lb.)*
+ *Brandy or sherry*
+ 4 *oz. mushrooms, sliced*
+ 1 *medium onion, peeled and sliced*
+ 1 *lb. potato puff pastry*
+ *Egg for brushing on*

Potato Puff Pastry

Mix 11 oz. S.R. (self-rising) flour, 5 oz. mashed potato, ½ teaspoonful salt. Add 6 tablespoonfuls water to make dough. Knead. Leave in fridge for 10 minutes. Roll into strip approx. 18 in. by 5 in., dot 8 oz. butter over two-thirds pastry. Fold into three, turn and roll out. Repeat. Place in fridge for 30 minutes. Turn and roll three more times. Leave in fridge for 2–3 hours.

Fillet of Beef

Trim meat, brush with brandy and brown in greased fry-pan. Place meat in oven for 10 minutes, remove. Prepare vegetables— fry mushrooms and onion until soft; drain off excess liquid. Roll out pastry into a rectangle about ⅛ in. thick, spread mushrooms and onion in centre and brush round the edges of pastry with water. Place meat on top of mushrooms, fold to make a parcel, cut sides of pastry at an angle and straight across (reserve piece for decoration), press edges to seal. Place in roasting-tin, brush with egg. Roll out pastry trimmings to make decorations, place on pastry and brush with egg. Bake for 40 minutes.

CORNISH PASTIES

Cooking time: 15 minutes at 400° F. (Gas Mark 6) 4 Pasties
30 minutes at 350° F. (Gas Mark 4)

+ *8 oz. potato pastry*
+ *12 oz. floury potatoes, peeled and diced*
+ *8 oz. best steak, chopped*
+ *Small piece of kidney, chopped (optional)*
+ *1 swede or turnip, peeled and diced (optional)*
+ *1 onion, sliced*
+ *Egg or milk*

Potato pastry:

Rub 4 oz. butter into 5 oz. sieved S.R. flour until mixture
resembles fine breadcrumbs. Add ¼ teaspoonful salt and 3 oz.
mashed potato, using a fork to blend them into the mixture.
Leave to stand in refrigerator for an hour until absolutely cold.

Pasties:

Roll pastry out ¼ in. thick, cut into 4 rounds, using a saucer
as a guide. *Mix meat and vegetables with salt and pepper, divide
into 4 portions. Place in centre of pastry rounds, damp edges and
draw together sealing well, flute edges with finger and thumb.
Brush with beaten egg or milk, make slits for steam to escape,
place on greased baking-sheet and bake.

---

* Use scissors to chop meat.

SHRIMP POTATO BAKE

- ✦ 1 *lb. boiled new potatoes*
- ✦ *½ pint peeled shrimps*
- ✦ 2 *sliced hard-boiled eggs*
- ✦ 2 *oz. fresh breadcrumbs*
- ✦ *¼ pint single cream*
- ✦ 1–2 *oz. butter*
- ✦ *Salt and pepper*

Slice the potatoes about ¼ in. thick, place in a greased pie-dish. Cover with the shrimps, hard-boiled eggs and breadcrumbs. Pour cream over the top, dot with butter and bake in a hot oven, 400° F. or Gas Mark 6 for 15–20 minutes. Sprinkle with freshly chopped parsley just before serving.

IRISH STEW

Serves 4
Cooking time: 1½–2 hours

- ✦ 2 *lb. potatoes, peeled*
- ✦ 1 *lb. neck or breast of mutton, trimmed*
- ✦ 3 *medium onions, peeled and quartered*
- ✦ 3 *medium carrots, scraped and sliced*
- ✦ 1 *pint water*
- ✦ *Parsley, chopped*

Leave small potatoes whole, and cut large ones into quarters. Prepare the other vegetables. Cut meat into pieces. Place all the vegetables and meat in a saucepan, with the potatoes on top. Season with salt and pepper. Add the water, bring to boil, remove surface fat and cover. Simmer gently for 1½–2 hours or until the meat is tender. Pile the meat, onions and carrots in the centre of a hot serving-dish, and surround with the potatoes. Sprinkle parsley on top.

SWEET POTATO CAKE

Cooking time: 40 minutes at 375° F. (Gas Mark 5)

+ 1 *lb. potatoes, peeled and boiled*
+ 4 *oz. icing sugar*
+ 4 *oz. candied peel, shredded*
+ 2 *oz. butter, melted*
+ *Vanilla essence (optional)*
+ *A little sugar*
+ 2 *eggs*

Sieve potatoes into a basin, add sugar, peel, butter and a little flavouring, such as vanilla if wished. Separate eggs. Mix in the beaten yolks and then the whisked whites. Add a little milk if the potatoes appear dry. Put the mixture into a greased lined 8 in. sandwich tin, smooth it on top and bake until browned. Sprinkle with sugar.

Serve hot or cold at teatime.

SECTION TWO
Meat Recipes

When I've been away on my travels, I've often noticed how so many people when they go on holiday go, not to see the country, but to stay in standardized hotels overlooking standardized beaches with standardized people on them, perhaps taking a small amount of time off from this hectic life to visit the local shops to buy some standardized souvenirs (made in Japan).

Ask them what they ate when they were abroad and they'll give you a list of dishes which pretty closely resemble what they'd eat at home. 'I couldn't eat any of that foreign rubbish,' they'll say. I can tell you, it's all rather depressing.

People seem afraid of strange-sounding foods. But to those people, I want to say put your fears at rest. The foods of other lands may seem strange to the ear, but basically the ingredients are the same, just put together in a different way.

Take our first recipe, the Moroccan Tajine. This is a dish that can be made with chicken or lamb, and either way it is served with almonds and spread over with a mixture of honey and raisins. We're going to make it with lamb.

Moroccan meals consist chiefly of well cooked meats simmering in spiced sauces, heavy with oil and butter. Sauces in which ginger and pepper mingle with honey and sugar. In their cookery the role of vegetables is reduced to a discreet accompaniment.

This tradition of cookery was brought to Morocco from the Orient and integrated with the simple meals of the Berbers. Its flowering is found in Fez, which is the gastronomic capital of the country.

The Moroccans, of course, eat their meals with their fingers, so that is how you should eat this dish when you've cooked it. It is also the custom for the host to tear off succulent pieces of the meat for the guests, all seated cross-legged on a rug on the floor. Serve plenty of bread with the tajine, so that you can hold the hot meat in a piece of bread and at the same time the delicious juices and sauce are absorbed in the bread.

To those of you who think eating in this way—with the fingers that is—is unhygienic, let me remind you that the Moroccans wash their hands very thoroughly before and after the meal, and that there are probably fewer germs on their fingers than are on the forks which come straight from a drawer, where they've been gathering dust, to the table and then to the mouth—you can imagine what that sounds like to a Moroccan!

Anyway to our first dish.

MOROCCAN TAJINE

Serves 4

+ 1 *leg of lamb*
+ 1 *medium onion*
+ 1 *clove garlic*
+ *Pepper*
+ *Saffron*
+ *Salt*
+ *Oil*

Cover the bottom of a large pan with about ¼ in. oil. Heat gradually with coarsely chopped onion, crushed garlic clove, add 1 teaspoon each of saffron, pepper and salt. When hot add the lamb, baste well and cover with tight-fitting lid. Leave on slow heat for ½ hour, basting occasionally. Then add one cup of water and leave to cook for one hour or more.

Place lamb in baking-tray with a little of the juice in which it has been cooked and put in a moderate oven (Gas Mark 5) to brown. This takes about 5 minutes for each side.

Sauce:

Soak 4 oz. raisins in water for 10 minutes. Heat in a saucepan ½ in. oil, 4 coarsely chopped onions, the raisins, 1 heaped tablespoon cinnamon. Cook over a moderate heat, stirring frequently until the onions are soft and brown (approx. ½ hour). Add 2 tablespoons of honey to the mixture.

Presentation:

Serve the 'Tajine' on a large platter surrounded by the sauce. Decorate with 4 oz. whole, blanched almonds which have been fried gently in butter for a few minutes. This dish is traditionally served with plenty of bread.

DOLMADES

In Denmark they call it the Kaaldomer, in Greece it's Dolmades and they have names for it in Russia, Turkey and throughout central Europe. Basically, our next dish is cabbage leaves stuffed with meat and rice. It can be almost any kind of meat, and you could use vine leaves to wrap the meat in if you're feeling exotic!

Three or four of these tasty tit-bits per person makes a delicious first course, or serve more if it is to be your main dish.

DOLMADES

Serves 6

+ 1 *large cabbage*
+ 2 *tablespoons long-grain rice*
+ ½ *pint milk*
+ 8 *oz. minced pork*
+ 8 *oz. minced veal*
+ 1 *teaspoon salt*
+ 5 *eggs, separated*
+ ¼ *teaspoon pepper*
+ 1 *medium onion, grated*
+ ½ *pint beef stock*
+ 3 *tablespoons black treacle*
+ ½ *teaspoon cornflour*
+ 12 *oz.* (1½ *cups*) *long-grain rice*
+ 1½ *pints* (3 *cups*) *water*
+ 1½ *teaspoons salt*
+ 2 *oz. butter*
+ 1 *tablespoon fresh chopped parsley*
+ 1 *tablespoon fresh chopped chives or spring onion*

Cut the core from cabbage, cook in salted water for 15 minutes, drain, cool slightly, and remove 24 large leaves. Simmer 2 tablespoons rice in milk for 40 minutes, cool. Mix pork, veal and salt together. Gradually beat in egg-whites, one at a time, beating vigorously after each addition. Slowly beat in the rice mixture and make a creamy filling (use electric beater if possible). Stir in pepper and onion. Preheat oven to 375° F. or Gas Mark 5. Cut the thick stalk from cabbage leaves. Place a tablespoon of meat filling on each leaf. Roll leaf over once, turn sides over filling, then fold each to the end of the leaf, completely enclosing filling. Arrange rolls in buttered baking-pan (approx. 9 in. by 12½ in.). Add stock and spread each roll with treacle. Bake for 30 minutes. Turn each roll and bake for 30 minutes longer. Put rice, water and salt into a saucepan. Bring to the boil and stir once. Lower heat to simmer. Cover and cook for about 15 minutes or until water is absorbed.

Sauce:

Remove rolls from pan and stir into remaining liquid cornflour mixed with 1 tablespoon water. Cook over direct heat, stirring for two minutes.

When rice is cooked fork in butter and herbs.

Serve cabbage rolls on a bed of herbed rice and pour sauce over.

Argentina—Revolutions, gauchos, Peronistas, cattle, lots of cattle. It's not really surprising that most of the really good recipes to come out of the Argentine make use of beef. And they have such romantic names too—'Matambre Arrollado' or Hunger Killer, 'Ninos Envueltos' or Swaddled Babes, 'Puchero', Boiled Beef to you and I.

MATAMBRE ARROLLADO
(Hunger Killer)

Serves 4

✦ 1½ slice (1½ lb.) Beef—Silverside or Chuck Steak

Marinade:
✦ ¼ pint corn oil
✦ ¼ pint white wine (medium sweet)
✦ 3 fluid oz. vinegar
✦ 2 garlic cloves, chopped
✦ 2 bayleaves
✦ ¼ teaspoon chopped parsley
✦ Salt and pepper

Filling:
✦ 1 tablespoon chopped parsley
✦ 1 tablespoon spring onion or chives, chopped
✦ 8 oz. raw carrot, coarsely grated
✦ 4 bacon rashers, stretched thinly

Other ingredients:
✦ 1 medium onion, sliced
✦ 1 stick celery, chopped
✦ Celery curls
✦ Sliced cucumber ⎫ as garnishes
✦ Sliced tomatoes ⎭

Trim the beef, lay flat on the table and beat it as flat as possible. Place in a shallow dish. Combine all ingredients for the marinade and pour over the beef. Cover and leave for up to 6 hours.

Beef Stroganoff with
Pimento Rice
(p. 82)

Rice-Stuffed
Green Peppers
(p. 97)

Manhattan Vichyssoise
(p. 3)

Coquilles St. Jacques
(p. 7)

Chocolate Hazelnut Gateau (p. 119)

Vincent Price with a glass of Café Napoleon

Coffee Walnut Gateau (p. 170)

Orange Rose Creams (p. 123)

Vincent Price putting finishing touches to Moroccan Tajine

Terrine of Pork (p. 60)

Seafood Rice Casserole (p. 85)

Pommes de Terre Savoyarde (p. 2)

Farmhouse Chicken Casserole (p. 9)

Lamb Salad Amondine (p. 45)

Apple and Citrus Soufflé (p. 121)

Creamy Kipper Scallops (p. 133)

Summertime Flan (p. 151)

Baked Ham in Common Crust (p. 56)

Ayrshire Poacher's Roll (p. 58)

Vincent Price with (left to right) Nasi Goreng, Gulfcoast Salad,
Hawaiian Chicken and Long Grain Rice

Prawn and Cheese Savoury (p. 160)

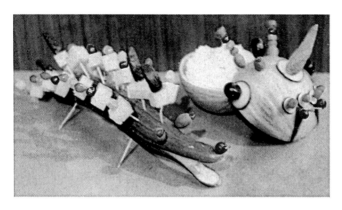

Crocodile Cucumber and Melon Monster (p. 147)

Vincent Price in Thames Television series—COOKING PRICE-WISE

Lift beef onto the table and cover with the filling ingredients. Pour over some of the marinade. Roll the beef tightly and secure with string. Place in a pan. Just cover with boiling water. Add onion, celery and salt, cover the pan and simmer for about 1½ hours for Silverside, or 2 hours for Chuck Steak.

Leave meat in the cooking liquid until cold. Lift out, remove string and slice. Serve garnished with celery curls, slices of cucumber and tomatoes.

APRICOT STUFFED SHOULDER

✦ 1 *shoulder of lamb*

Apricot Stuffing:

✦ 1 *(15 oz.) can apricot halves*

✦ 1 *small onion, finely chopped*

✦ 1 *oz. butter*

✦ 1 *tablespoon parsley, chopped*

✦ 2 *oz. fresh white breadcrumbs*

✦ *Salt and pepper*

Bone the shoulder of lamb (or ask the butcher to do so). Drain the apricots and reserve the juice. Keep 5 or 6 pieces of fruit for garnish and chop the remainder. Fry the onion in the butter until soft but not brown. Mix with the chopped apricots, parsley, breadcrumbs, salt and pepper. Stuff the shoulder with the apricot stuffing, roll up and tie securely with string. Place in a roasting tin and pour the reserved apricot juice over the lamb. Roast in a moderate oven 350° F. (Gas Mark 4) for 40–45 minutes per pound, basting occasionally. Serve garnished with the reserved apricot halves.

NINOS ENVUELTOS
(Swaddled Babes)

Serves 6

✦ 1½ lb. beef cut into thin slices—Topside or Silverside

Stuffing:
✦ ½ onion, chopped
✦ 2 oz. butter
✦ 3 oz. white breadcrumbs
✦ 1 oz. Parmesan cheese, grated
✦ Salt and pepper
✦ 2 tablespoons celery, finely chopped (optional)
✦ 1 egg, beaten

For braising:
✦ 2 onions, chopped
✦ 4 tablespoons oil
✦ 4 tomatoes, peeled and chopped
✦ 2 bayleaves
✦ 4 tablespoons sweet red wine
✦ ½ pint stock
✦ Mashed potato (as accompaniment)

To make the stuffing, colour onion in the butter. Remove from heat and mix in the breadcrumbs, cheese, parsley, seasoning, celery and beaten egg to bind the mixture. Lay slices of Argentine beef out flat and sprinkle with salt and pepper. Roll them with a rolling-pin until just about paper thin. Place some stuffing on each steak. Roll up and secure with cocktail sticks.

For braising, colour the onions in heated oil. Add tomatoes and soften them. Brown the beef rolls all over. Add bayleaves, wine and stock. Cover and simmer for ¾ to 1 hour until quite tender.

Lift out the rolls, remove sticks and keep hot. Boil liquid to reduce quantity slightly and strain over the beef rolls before serving. Decorate serving-dish with piped creamy mashed potato, or serve separately.

BAKED PORK CHOPS COUNTRY STYLE

Serves 4

+ *4 spare rib pork chops*
+ *Clove garlic*
+ *Few juniper berries (optional)*
+ *1½ lb. potatoes, sliced thinly*
+ *1 onion, sliced*
+ *1 oz. fat*
+ *Salt, pepper, nutmeg*
+ *4 oz. cheap bacon pieces*
+ *Small glass white wine or cider*

Put a sliver of garlic and two juniper berries near the bone of each chop. Brown the chops in the fat. Arrange half the potatoes and onion in an earthenware casserole and season with salt, pepper and nutmeg. Place chops on top, cover with remaining potatoes and onion and season again. Cover with bacon, pour over wine or cider and cover with foil and lid. Cook in very slow oven, 300° F. (Gas Mark 2) for about 3 hours. Before serving, pour off surplus fat and brown for a few minutes without lid.

PUCHERO
(Boiled Beef)

Puchero:

✦ 3 *lb. joint beef—Chuck Steak, Silverside or Brisket*

✦ 4 *carrots, peeled and thickly sliced*

✦ 2 *leeks, trimmed and thickly sliced*

✦ 2 *small turnips, peeled and chopped*

✦ 2 *or* 3 *corn on the cob, chopped*

✦ 1 *green pepper, chopped*

✦ 1 *onion, chopped*

✦ 1 *tomato, peeled and chopped*

✦ 1½ *to* 2 *lb. potatoes, peeled and chopped*

Other ingredients:

✦ 1 *cabbage, quartered*

✦ 1 *lb. sweet potato, peeled and chopped*

✦ 1 *lb. vegetable marrow, peeled, de-seeded and chopped*

✦ ¾ *lb. lean bacon joint*

✦ ½ *lb. black pudding, thickly sliced*

✦ ½ *lb. chick peas*, previously soaked in water*

✦ *Salt and pepper*

Half fill a large saucepan with water, add salt (2 teaspoons to 2 pints water) and bring to the boil. Tie beef neatly, place in the water, cover and simmer gently for 30 minutes. Add the carrots,

---

* Chick peas are obtainable at Health Food shops. They may be replaced by long-grain rice which should be cooked separately in stock taken from the Puchero towards the end of cooking time.

Other ingredients are cooked separately so that their flavour does not penetrate the Puchero stock, and to prevent the black pudding from darkening it.

leeks, turnips, corn, pepper, onion and tomato and continue simmering for 1 hour. Add potatoes and cook gently for a further 20 to 30 minutes when beef will be tender.

Meanwhile, place prepared cabbage, sweet potato, marrow, bacon, black pudding and chick peas in another saucepan, add seasoning and cover with boiling water. Cover and simmer for about 1 hour. Lift out bacon, cut into shreds and replace in the pan to heat through again.

Add the Puchero to the other ingredients and serve accompanied by a raw vegetable salad.

LAMB À L'ORANGE

Serves 4

+ 1 *small onion, very finely chopped*
+ 1 *tablespoon oil*
+ 1 *large orange*
+ 1 *tablespoon redcurrant jelly*
+ ½ *pint stock*
+ ½ *teaspoon dry mustard*
+ ½ *teaspoon caster sugar*
+ *Pinch cayenne pepper*
+ 1 *tablespoon cornflour*
+ 12 *oz. lamb from a cooked leg or shoulder*

Fry the onion gently in the oil until soft but not brown. Grate the orange rind; cut three fine slices from the orange. Trim the pith and reserve for garnish. Squeeze the juice from the remainder of the orange and add to the onion with the orange rind, redcurrant jelly and stock. Bring to the boil, reduce heat and cook stirring for 5 minutes. Blend the mustard, sugar, pepper and cornflour together with 2 tablespoons of cold water and stir into the orange sauce. Slice the lamb, add to the sauce and bring to the boil. Reduce the heat and simmer for 15 minutes. Serve garnished with the reserved orange slices.

BIFES DE LOMO RELLENOS
(Stuffed Fillet Steaks)

Serves 4

♦ 4 *Fillet Steaks, 1 in. thick*

Stuffing:
♦ 2 *oz. lean bacon, chopped*
♦ ½ *hard-boiled egg, chopped*
♦ 2 *teaspoons capers, chopped*
♦ 1 *oz. cheese, finely chopped*
♦ ½ *teaspoon made mustard*
♦ *Salt and pepper*
♦ ½ *egg, beaten*

Sauce:
♦ 1½ *oz. butter*
♦ 1 *medium onion, chopped*
♦ 1 *teaspoon parsley, chopped*
♦ 4 *oz. mushrooms, thinly sliced*
♦ 1 *medium tomato, peeled and sliced*
♦ 4 *tablespoons sweet red wine*
♦ ¼ *pint stock*
♦ 2 *teaspoons cornflour*
♦ 4 *tablespoons single cream*

Other ingredients:
♦ Half the contents of a 3-oz. jar maraschino cherries, drained. 1 dessertspoon made mustard. Parsley sprigs for garnish.

Cut a 'pocket' through one side of each steak. Mix all ingredients for stuffing together with beaten egg to bind. Fill each 'pocket' with stuffing and secure openings with cocktail sticks. Wrap steaks in foil and bake for 20 to 25 minutes at 425° F. (Gas Mark 7).

To make the sauce, heat butter and cook the onion in it until coloured. Stir in parsley, mushrooms, tomato, wine and half the stock. Blend cornflour with remaining stock, stir into sauce and cook 2 to 3 minutes. Stir in the cream away from heat.

Arrange steaks on a serving-dish. Pour sauce over and keep hot in the oven. Garnish with parsley sprigs before serving. Heat cherries with mustard and serve with the steaks.

EMPANADAS SALTERAS
(Meat Pasties from Salta)

Makes 18–20

Pink Lard:
+ 2 *teaspoons paprika*
+ 2 *tablespoons boiling water*
+ 4 *oz. lard*

Filling:
+ 1 *oz. pink lard*
+ 1 *lb. minced beef—Chuck Steak, Flank or Brisket*
+ 2 *tablespoons water*
+ 2 *onions, chopped and blanched*
+ 3 *oz. cooked potato, diced small*
+ 3 *oz. raisins, chopped*
+ 2 *hard-boiled eggs, chopped*
+ ½ *teaspoon chillies, crushed*
+ 2 *teaspoons parsley, chopped*
+ *Salt and pepper*

Pastry:
+ 1 *lb. plain flour*
+ 3 *to* 4 *oz. pink lard*
+ 8 *to* 9 *fluid oz. warm, salted water*

Other ingredients:
+ *Sifted icing sugar*

To make pink lard, place paprika in a saucepan. Pour on the water, add lard and stir over a low heat until lard melts. Strain through muslin to remove pepper grains.

Blanch the onions by just covering them with cold water and bringing them to the boil for 2 minutes. Strain them and chop.

To make the filling, put pink lard (about 1 tablespoon while soft) in a saucepan to heat. Mix beef with water to separate the pieces, then brown all over in the lard. Remove from heat and mix in all remaining ingredients for filling. Add salt and pepper to taste. Leave until cold.

To make pastry, place flour in a heap on the table and make a 'well' in the centre. Pour cooled, soft lard into the 'well' with some of the water and gradually work flour into the liquid, adding more liquid as needed to make a dough that is soft but firm to the touch. Knead the dough thoroughly without extra flour on the table. Air bubbles will begin to appear in it when it is ready.

Roll out the dough very thinly (no flour is needed) and cut out 18 to 20 rounds the size of an average saucer.

Damp the edges with water and spoon some filling on to each round. Fold pastry over to meet opposite edge, making a semicircle. Tuck the two edges up and over the Empanadas, making tiny 'pleats' at intervals to make a firm, decorative border.

Fry in deep fat, a few at a time, turning once or twice until browned. Drain on kitchen paper. Dredge with icing sugar and serve hot.

Empanadas may also be brushed with beaten egg and baked on greased trays for 15 minutes at 425° F. (Gas Mark 7). As an alternative they can be brushed with egg and sprinkled with granulated sugar before baking.

For cocktail savouries, make tiny Empanadas to serve hot or cold.

TOURNEDOS VICTOR HUGO

Serves 4

- ✦ 4 *slices beef—Fillet Steak*
- ✦ *Oil*
- ✦ *Salt*

Neapolitan Tomato Sauce:
- ✦ 1 *large clove of garlic*
- ✦ 4 *tablespoons olive oil*
- ✦ 2 *tablespoons tomato paste*
- ✦ 2 *tablespoons warm water*
- ✦ 1 (1 *lb.*) *can tomatoes*
- ✦ ½ *teaspoon salt*
- ✦ *Ground black pepper*
- ✦ ½ *teaspoon sugar*
- ✦ ½ *teaspoon dried basil*

Sauce Béarnaise:
- ✦ ½ *teaspoon finely chopped shallot*
- ✦ ½ *teaspoon dried tarragon*
- ✦ 1 *teaspoon dried chervil*
- ✦ ⅛ *teaspoon cayenne pepper*
- ✦ ½ *teaspoon salt*
- ✦ *Ground black pepper*
- ✦ 2 *tablespoons tarragon vinegar OR* 1 *tablespoon tarragon and* 1 *tablespoon white wine*
- ✦ 2 *large egg yolks*
- ✦ 3 *oz. butter*
- ✦ 4 *button mushrooms, fried in butter, for garnish*

To Make Tomato Sauce:

Squash the clove of garlic without cutting it and heat in the oil without browning. Remove garlic. Dilute tomato paste with the warm water and add to the oil. Remove cores from tomatoes and chop up roughly. Add to tomato paste. Stir in the seasonings, sugar and basil. Bring sauce to the boil and simmer gently, uncovered, for 20–30 minutes, stirring occasionally.

To Make Sauce Béarnaise:

Put shallot, tarragon, chervil, seasonings and liquid into a small saucepan and bubble until reduced by two-thirds. Remove from heat and cool a little. Stir in the egg yolks. Return to a very gentle heat and beat in the butter, piece by piece, until the sauce is thick and smooth.

After making sauces, tie each tournedo into a neat round. Brush with oil, and sprinkle with salt. Grill under a fierce heat for approximately 3 minutes on each side. The meat should be rare in the centre.

Garnish each steak with a button mushroom and serve on a bed of Sauce Béarnaise. Serve Tomato Sauce separately.

WELLINGTON SALAD

+ *12 oz. lamb from a cooked leg or shoulder*
+ *1–2 teaspoons orange liqueur (optional)*
+ *3 oranges, peeled*
+ *2 sticks celery, finely chopped*
+ *2 oz. desiccated coconut*
+ *1 teaspoon curry powder*
+ *4 tablespoons mayonnaise*
+ *1 lettuce, washed*

Cut the lamb into ½ in. cubes and sprinkle with the liqueur. Cut 3–4 slices from one of the oranges and reserve for decoration. Chop the remaining oranges and add to the lamb with the celery. Mix the coconut, curry powder and mayonnaise together. Add to the lamb mixture and mix well. Arrange the lettuce leaves on a serving-plate and pile the salad on top. Garnish with the reserved orange slices.

LAMB SALAD AMONDINE

Serves 4

+ 1 *lb. shoulder or leg lamb, cooked*
+ 2 *sticks celery, chopped*
+ 2 *oz. flaked almonds*
+ 1 *small red pepper, de-seeded and chopped*
+ 4 *tablespoons mayonnaise*
+ 1 *pinch celery salt*
+ 1 *lettuce, washed*

Cut the lamb into small pieces. Add celery, almonds, and pepper. Mix together celery salt and mayonnaise and toss lamb and vegetables in the mixture; chill. Make cup shapes from the lettuce leaves. Pile the lamb salad on these cups and serve immediately.

CASSEROLE OF LAMB WITH CIDER

Serves 6–8

+ 2 *lb. shoulder without bone*
+ *Flour*
+ 2 *oz. butter*
+ 2 *small onions, chopped*
+ ½ *clove garlic, chopped*
+ 2 *tablespoons parsley, chopped*
+ ¼ *pint each stock and cider*
+ 1 *tablespoon Worcester sauce*
+ 1 *level teaspoon salt, pepper*

Cut meat into cubes and coat with flour. Fry in the butter until browned on all sides. Put in casserole dish with the onion, garlic and parsley. Pour stock and cider into the frying-pan and stir till boiling. Add Worcester sauce and seasoning and simmer for 5 minutes. Pour over meat, cover dish and simmer for 1 hour in a slow oven, 330° F. (Gas Mark 3).

CARBONNADE OF BEEF

Serves 4-6

- ✦ *2½ lb. Chuck beef*
- ✦ *1½ oz. seasoned flour*
- ✦ *3 oz. best dripping*
- ✦ *1 heaped tablespoon tomato purée*
- ✦ *1 level teaspoon made mustard*
- ✦ *1 pint brown ale*
- ✦ *1 bayleaf*
- ✦ *few sprigs of parsley*
- ✦ *salt and pepper*
- ✦ *2 small onions*

Cut meat into 1 in. cubes and toss in seasoned flour. Melt fat in a pan and fry meat and onions until lightly browned. Add tomato purée and mustard and blend in beer. Add bayleaf and parsley. Season. Bring to the boil, then simmer for 2½ hours. Alternatively, transfer to a casserole and simmer at 325° F., or Gas Mark 3, for 2½ hours.

BREAST OF LAMB WITH GREEN HERBS

Serves 6–8

+ *2 breasts of lamb, boned*
+ *2 oz. butter*
+ *1 large onion, finely chopped*
+ *1½–2 oz. green herbs, such as parsley, mint, watercress*
+ *1 egg, beaten with 2 tablespoons milk*
+ *2 slices of bread without crust*
+ *Salt, pepper, sugar*

Trim excess fat from meat. Cook onion gently in butter until transparent. Chop herbs. Soak the bread in egg and milk and mash well. Mix onions, herbs and bread and season with salt, pepper and ½ teaspoon sugar. Divide mixture between the two breasts, spread it out evenly, roll each of them up and tie with string. Roast in a hot oven, 450° F. (Gas Mark 8), for 1 hour. Use the bones for stock.

STUFFED LOIN CHOPS (Lamb)

Serves 4

+ *4 loin chops*
+ *2 lamb's kidneys*
+ *4 rashers of bacon*
+ *3 oz. dripping*

Skin and halve the kidneys, and take out the cores. Take the bones out of the chops and curl each one round half a kidney. Wrap a piece of bacon round the chop and fix in place with a skewer. Fry very gently until cooked through in the dripping.

MOUSSAKA

Serves 4

- ✦ 1 *lb. aubergines, thinly sliced*
- ✦ *Oil for frying*
- ✦ 2 *large onions, thinly sliced*
- ✦ 1 *clove garlic, crushed*
- ✦ 1 *lb. lamb, minced*
- ✦ 1 (15 *oz.) can tomatoes*
- ✦ 2 *tablespoons tomato purée*
- ✦ *Salt and pepper*
- ✦ 2 *eggs*
- ✦ 1 (5 *oz.) carton single cream*
- ✦ 2 *oz. Lancashire cheese, grated or crumbled*
- ✦ 1 *oz. Parmesan cheese, grated*

Fry the aubergines in oil for 3–4 minutes; remove and drain well. Fry the onions and garlic in 1 tablespoon of oil until pale golden brown. Add the lamb and cook for about 10 minutes, stirring occasionally. Add the tomatoes and tomato pureé and mix well. Bring to the boil and simmer for 20–25 minutes. Season with salt and pepper. Arrange alternate layers of aubergines and the lamb mixture in a large soufflé dish or shallow casserole. Bake in a moderate oven, 350°F. (Gas Mark 4) for 35–40 minutes. Meanwhile, beat the eggs and cream together and stir in the cheese. Pour onto the moussaka and return to the oven for a further 15–20 minutes until the topping is firm, well risen and golden brown.

CUTLETS REFORMÉ

Serves 4

- ✦ 8 *lamb cutlets*
- ✦ 1 *oz. flour, seasoned*
- ✦ *Egg and breadcrumbs for coating*
- ✦ *Oil for deep frying*

Reformé Sauce:
- ✦ 2 *oz. butter*
- ✦ 2 *oz. streaky bacon, chopped*
- ✦ 1 *shallot or small onion, chopped*
- ✦ 1 *large tomato, quartered*
- ✦ 1 *small carrot, sliced*
- ✦ 2 *oz. plain flour*
- ✦ 1 *pint brown stock*
- ✦ 2 *teaspoons mushroom ketchup (optional)*
- ✦ 1 *bouquet garni*
- ✦ *Pepper and salt*
- ✦ 1 *tablespoon redcurrant jelly*
- ✦ 1 *tablespoon port*

Trim and wipe the cutlets. Dip them in seasoned flour and coat with egg and breadcrumbs. To make the sauce, melt the butter in a saucepan. Add the bacon and fry slowly for 10 minutes. Add the sliced vegetables and sauté until golden brown, stirring occasionally. Add the flour and continue to fry slowly until a rich brown colour. Add the stock, mushroom ketchup and bouquet garni and simmer, covered, for 40 minutes. Skim and sieve the sauce. Add the redcurrant jelly and heat gently until the jelly dissolves. Stir in the port and check the seasoning. To fry the crumbed cutlets, heat a pan of cooking oil to a temperature of 380° F. (at this temperature the oil is slightly smoking). Place the cutlets in the hot oil and fry for 1 minute. Turn off the heat and allow the cutlets to continue cooking in the oil for a further 5 minutes. Drain well and place a cutlet frill on the end of each cutlet and arrange on a serving dish. Serve the cutlets with the Reformé Sauce and creamed potatoes.

CHILI-CON-CARNE

Serves 4

+ *4 oz. onion, peeled and chopped*
+ *1 clove garlic, crushed*
+ *1 oz. fat*
+ *1 lb. lamb, minced*
+ *1 tablespoon paprika*
+ *1 tablespoon chili-con-carne seasoning*
+ *1 tablespoon tomato purée*
+ *1 (8 oz.) can tomatoes*
+ *1 teaspoon sugar*
+ *Salt and pepper*
+ *1 (8 oz.) can red kidney beans, drained and rinsed*

Fry the onion and garlic slowly in the fat until soft but not brown. Add the lamb and cook for 10 minutes, until brown. Stir in the paprika, chili-con-carne seasoning and tomato pureé. Add the tomatoes and sugar, and season to taste with salt and pepper. Cover and simmer gently for 30 minutes until tender. Add the kidney beans and continue to cook for 5 minutes to heat through. Serve with rice and a salad.

GOULASH

Serves 6

- ✦ 2 *lb. chuck steak*
- ✦ 1 *lb. onions, sliced*
- ✦ 3 *oz. lard*
- ✦ 1 *oz. paprika*
- ✦ 2 *tablespoons flour mixed with* 1 *teaspoon salt*
- ✦ 1 *lb. tomatoes, or* 1 *lb. can*
- ✦ *Glass red wine*
- ✦ ½–1 *pint stock*
- ✦ 1 *clove garlic and bouquet garni (sprig parsley and thyme and a bayleaf)*

Cut the meat into 1 in. cubes and roll them first in paprika and then in flour. Brown onions in the fat, and then brown meat on all sides. Add tomatoes, and wine and cook fiercely for a few minutes. Add any remaining flour and paprika, pour over enough stock to cover, add the garlic and the bouquet garni. Cover and cook very slowly on top of the stove or in the oven for about 2 hours. Parboil the potatoes, add them to the goulash and cook for a further 20 minutes to ½ hour.

GUARD OF HONOUR

+ *2 best ends of lamb, chined*
+ *Cherries*
+ *Cutlet frills*
+ *Watercress to garnish*

Trim the fat and skin from the ends of the rib bones so that
1 in. of bone protrudes. Stand the two joints close together in
a roasting tin so that the tips of the bones cross each other like
the swords in a guard of honour. Cover the bone tips with foil to
prevent them burning during cooking. Bake in a moderate oven,
350° F. (Gas Mark 4) for 1¼ hours. Remove the foil and place
on a hot serving-plate. Place alternate cherries and cutlet frills on
the bones and garnish with watercress.

LAMB KEBABS

For 4 kebabs allow:

✦ *1½ lb. leg or shoulder of lamb*

Marinade—

   ✦ *6 tablespoons olive oil*

   ✦ *6 tablespoons pineapple juice*

   ✦ *2 teaspoons lemon juice*

   ✦ *1 teaspoon Worcester sauce*

   ✦ *1 teaspoon chopped parsley*

   ✦ *1 onion, thinly sliced*

   ✦ *1 small carrot, grated*

   ✦ *8 small mushrooms*

   ✦ *4 slices streaky bacon*

   ✦ *8 pineapple cubes*

   ✦ *8 oz. long-grain rice*

   ✦ *1 small green pepper*

   ✦ *1 small red pepper*

Cut the meat into cubes. Mix all the ingredients for the marinade. Put in the meat and leave for at least 2 hours, stirring occasionally.

Wipe the mushrooms and remove the stalks. Cut each bacon rasher into halves. Add, with the pineapple, to the marinade for 5 minutes. Alternate the ingredients on the skewers having a cube of meat at each end and folding the pieces of bacon. Cook under a hot grill, turning as necessary and basting with the marinade.

Cook the rice and drain it. Prepare the peppers, cut into strips and simmer for 5 minutes. Add to the rice, with a little of the strained marinade, if liked. Put on a heated dish and arrange the skewers across the top.

SECTION THREE
Bacon Recipes

It was the Romans who brought the idea of curing bacon to Britain. In fact, they had been salting flitches of bacon from about 200 B.C., and when they made their take-over bid for these islands, they brought their bacon technology with them.

Since then, bacon has become one of the most typical of British foods. Indeed, it was the British who invented what is known as the Wiltshire cure—a method of curing bacon which has been adopted by every bacon-curing country of the world.

It was the Victorian English who, at the height of their imperial greatness, developed the British breakfast—eggs and bacon. It's not a dish you can avoid while travelling in Britain.

The Victorians also produced Mrs. Beaton—that magnificent lady who has been writing her posthumous cookery books ever since she died at an early age—many years ago. In fact, it is with one of her recipes that I want to start this chapter.

It's called Gammon in Common Crust. Now gammon is the prime cut of bacon, and it's naturally the most expensive. However, for this dish you can equally well use one of the less expensive cuts such as collar, or forehock. It really amazes me why these more economical cuts are not widely used—they really do taste just as good if cooked properly. I suppose the reason is ignorance on the part of the public and the vendor's natural desire to sell the most expensive cut, and thereby make more profit. So be it!

The idea behind this recipe is to use the common crust, or pastry, as a wrapping for the meat. This draws out the salt from the bacon while keeping in the flavour.

Using crust in this way existed long before tinfoil, and is still the best way of wrapping a large joint of bacon.

BAKED HAM OR GAMMON IN A COMMON CRUST

Serves 6

+ 1 *ham or 3½–4 lb. piece of gammon*
+ 1 *lb. plain flour*
+ 5 *oz. lard*
+ ¼ *pint water*

Boil water in saucepan. Put flour through sieve and make a hole in the centre. When water is boiling add lard and when this has melted pour it quickly into the flour. Beat well with a wooden spoon. Knead mixture until smooth. Leave to stand for 15 minutes.

Roll out and encase ham or piece of gammon in it, carefully sealing it. Place in a baking-tin in a moderate oven (Gas Mark 4) and allow 25 minutes per pound and 25 minutes over.

Take off crust and serve hot or cold. Serve with Cumberland Sauce.

Cumberland Sauce

+ *Juice and rind of 1 orange*
+ *4 tablespoons redcurrant jelly*
+ *Juice of 1 lemon*
+ *1 glass of port*
+ *2 oz. halved glacé cherries*

Remove rind from the orange with a potato peeler. Cut into needle-like shreds and cook in boiling water until tender (about 5 minutes). Drain and rinse well. Heat redcurrant jelly until dissolved. Take off heat and stir in lemon and orange juice (strained) and port. When cold add orange rind and halved glacé cherries.

The Wiltshire cure is not the only cure, however, as all those of you who enjoy Virginia ham will know. Another, again, is the Ayrshire cure, from that part of Scotland famous for producing Robert Burns, and being the site of the Scottish Grand National.

It was, until comparatively recent times, a land of great rural poverty, and constant rebellions against the kings—be they of England or Scotland! It is to these stout fellows that I dedicate this next recipe, which is called the Ayrshire Poacher's Roll, or Apple and Spiced Ayrshire Roll to give it its more prosaic title. In Scotland they make it with a roll of the Ayrshire cured bacon, but as you may not be able to get hold of it in your local shops, you can use any of the cheaper rolled cuts you choose.

Incidentally, for the curious, the word 'poacher' in the name of this dish does not refer to a game-thief, but to one who 'poached' on the king's authority—a rebel, in other words.

You might also like to know that the Ayrshire cure, which is milder than other British cures, was just about the only thing that arch Britisher, Dr. Samuel Johnson, ever found to praise in Scotland!

AYRSHIRE POACHER'S ROLL

Serves 6

+ 3½−4 *lb. Ayrshire Roll or middle cut bacon joint*
+ 1 *oz. butter*
+ 2 *medium-sized cooking apples, peeled, cored and chopped*
+ ½ *small onion, peeled and finely chopped*
+ *Salt and black pepper*
+ ½ *level teaspoonful mixed spice*
+ 2 *teaspoons chopped parsley*
+ 2 *oz. raisins*
+ 2½ *oz. white breadcrumbs*
+ 1 *standard egg, beaten*

Soak bacon joint in water overnight. Form bacon round a jam-jar* and tie firmly. Cover with cold water in a saucepan and simmer for half the cooking time, allowing 25 minutes per pound and 25 minutes over. Remove and allow to cool slightly. Remove skin. Melt butter in a pan and sauté apple and onion for a few minutes, being careful not to let the apple get too soft. Drain, then mix with seasonings, mixed spice, parsley, raisins and breadcrumbs. Bind together with an egg. Remove jam-jar from joint and fill cavity with stuffing. Secure with fresh string if necessary. Place in a roasting-tin and roast in a moderately hot oven 375° F. (Gas Mark 5) for the rest of the cooking time. Cover stuffing with foil if it is getting too brown. Serve hot or cold and garnish with parsley.

To go with your bacon joints I want to put in a word for a little recipe of my own—Wilted Spinach Salad with Bacon Dressing. This is made with raw spinach.

---

* A long, thin jam-jar is best.

You know very few people make use of raw spinach, which is a pity because it's really quite delicious. Still, with this little recipe you can make up for all that. The dressing also demonstrates that bacon rashers are far more flexible than 'eggs and bacon' would suggest. Mind you, I don't expect you to make the dish for breakfast, either.

WILTED SPINACH SALAD WITH BACON DRESSING

Serves 4

+ 1 *lb. young spinach*
+ 6 *spring onions*
+ 1 *tablespoon salad oil*
+ ½ *clove garlic*
+ 3 *rashers bacon*
+ 1 *tablespoon sugar*
+ 1 *tablespoon tarragon vinegar*
+ 1 *tablespoon red wine vinegar*
+ 1 *egg*
+ *Salt and pepper*

Cut roots and tough stems from spinach. Wash thoroughly in cold water. Drain, shake out all moisture and tear into small pieces. Chop spring onions very finely and mix with spinach. Mash garlic and cover with salad oil. Leave to stand for 30 minutes. Discard garlic and trickle over the spinach and let stand. Sauté bacon until crisp. Cut into strips and drain on absorbent paper. Keep bacon fat. Beat together egg, sugar, vinegars. Pour slowly into bacon fat, stirring constantly until mixture has thickened slightly. Season with salt and pepper to taste. Pour over spinach mixture and toss well. Crumble bacon strips and sprinkle over salad.

Serve immediately.

TERRINE OF PORK

- ✦ 6 *oz. streaky bacon rashers*
- ✦ 1 *lb. minced pork*
- ✦ *½ lb. pork sausage meat*
- ✦ 4 *oz. rolled oats*
- ✦ *Rind and juice of half lemon*
- ✦ 1 *teaspoon salt*
- ✦ *½ teaspoon seasonall*
- ✦ *½ teaspoon sage*
- ✦ *¼ teaspoon black pepper*
- ✦ 1 *grated onion*
- ✦ 1 *beaten egg*

Mix together all the ingredients except the rashers. De-rind and place the rashers on a board, then 'stretch' them by stroking length-wise gently with a dinner knife. Arrange in a 2-lb. loaf tin. Carefully press the meat mixture into the tin and level off the top. Cover with foil and put in a tin of water. Bake for 1½ hours at 350° F. (Gas Mark 4). When cooked, place weight on top and leave overnight. Turn out, slice and serve with salad.

Most farms in the British countryside used to have their own beehives, and honey used to be very widely used in country cookery. Modern bottling and distribution have made honey available to us all now, so it's a good idea to make use of it where possible in our cookery. This recipe 'Honey Baked Bacon' is a delightful way of combining bacon with honey. To make it you should use a middle gammon or corner gammon cut.

HONEY BAKED BACON

1¼ lb. joint serves 4

+ *Piece of bacon for boiling. Middle gammon or corner gammon are suitable for this recipe.*
+ *1 bayleaf*
+ *Pepper*
+ *1 small onion, skinned*
+ *2 tablespoons clear honey*
+ *½ teacup hot water*

Leave bacon to soak in cold water for 4 hours (or overnight). If packeted then follow instructions on label. Drain. Put into pan and cover with fresh water. Add the bayleaf, pepper and onion. Bring to the boil then simmer for 20 minutes per pound or until tender. Drain and remove rind while joint is hot. Turn on oven; set at moderate 275° F. (Gas Mark 5). Put bacon in a meat-tin. Mix honey with the hot water and pour over bacon. Cook for 30 minutes, basting twice during cooking.

This is delicious hot with sweet-n-sour red cabbage (chopped and sautéed in a little butter, vinegar and sugar, with added sultanas or apple pieces). If serving cold, serve with white cabbage and fresh orange salad tossed in an oil and vinegar dressing in which a little castor sugar has been well dissolved.

Note: Sweet or mild cure bacon requires no soaking.

PROVENÇAL BACON CASSEROLE

Serves 6–8

+ 3½–4 *lb. joint prime collar bacon, boned and rolled*
+ ½ *pint white wine*
+ *Water to cover*
+ ¾ *lb. button onions, peeled*
+ 2 *oz. butter*
+ 1 *lb. tomatoes, peeled and seeded and chopped*
+ 1 *level teaspoon oregano*
+ 4 *cloves garlic*
+ 2 *tablespoons dried breadcrumbs*

Soak joint overnight in cold water. Place in a saucepan with wine and cold water and simmer for half the cooking time, allowing 25 minutes per pound and 25 minutes over. Drain joint and remove the skin. Place on a large piece of foil in an ovenproof dish. Blanch onions for 10 minutes then drain. Melt butter in a pan and sauté onions until lightly golden. Add tomatoes and oregano and simmer gently for 10 minutes. Cut each clove of garlic into 4 strips and spike the bacon joint with them. Brush with a little melted butter and sprinkle with breadcrumbs. Surround the joint with the onion and tomato mixture and seal the foil to enclose it. Bake at 375° F. (Gas Mark 5) for remaining cooking time. Fold back foil and serve hot.

QUICHE LORRAINE

+ 8 *oz. small streaky bacon rashers, rinded*
+ 6 *oz. shortcrust pastry*
+ 1 *oz. butter*
+ 1 *small onion, peeled and finely chopped*
+ 2 *eggs*
+ *Seasoning*
+ ¼ *pint double cream*
+ ¼ *pint milk*
+ 2½ *oz. Gruyère cheese, grated*

Roll out pastry and line an 8½ in. flan ring. Chop up half the bacon, melt butter and sauté onion and chopped bacon until soft. Drain. Beat together eggs, seasoning, cream and milk. Add cheese, onion and bacon. Pour mixture into flan case and bake in a hot oven 425° F. (Gas Mark 7) for 10 minutes. Arrange remaining bacon rashers in a spoke design on the flan and a bacon roll in the centre. Return to oven, reduced to 350° F. (Gas Mark 4) for about 40 minutes until set and golden brown.

CORNISH BACON PASTIES

Serves 6

- ✦ 6 *oz. streaky bacon rashers, rinded and chopped*
- ✦ 12 *oz. shortcrust pastry (12 oz. flour, 3 oz. margarine, 3 oz. lard)*
- ✦ ½ *lb. minced raw steak*
- ✦ 4 *oz. lamb's kidney, chopped*
- ✦ 1 *large onion, peeled and chopped*
- ✦ *Salt and pepper*
- ✦ ½ *teaspoon Worcester sauce*
- ✦ *Beaten egg to glaze*

Roll out pastry and cut into six 7-in. rounds. Mix the bacon, steak, kidney, onion, seasonings and Worcester sauce. Divide into six and place across the middle of each piece of pastry. Damp edges of pastry with water, bring together and seal tightly. Glaze with beaten egg and place on wetted baking-trays. Bake at 425° F. (Gas Mark 7) for 15 minutes then reduce to 350° F. (Gas Mark 4) for a further 40–45 minutes till golden brown and centre is cooked through.

Serve hot or cold.

APPLE AND ORANGE STUFFED BACON

Serves 6–8

+ 3½–4 lb. middle-cut bacon joint (or Ayrshire Roll)
+ 2 medium-sized cooking apples, peeled, cored and chopped
+ 1 oz. butter
+ Grated rind of ½ orange
+ Flesh of 2 oranges, chopped
+ 2 oz. soaked raisins
+ 3 oz. breadcrumbs
+ 1 egg, beaten
+ Salt and pepper
+ 1 orange for garnish

Soak the bacon joint in cold water overnight. Form bacon round a jam-jar* and tie firmly. Cover with cold water in a saucepan and simmer for half the cooking time, allowing 25 minutes per pound and 25 minutes over. Remove and allow to cool slightly. Remove the skin. Sauté apple in butter for 5 minutes; drain, then mix with the orange rind and flesh, raisins, breadcrumbs, egg and seasonings. Remove jam-jar and fill cavity with stuffing. Secure with fresh string if necessary. Place in a roasting-tin and roast in a moderately hot oven 375° F. (Gas Mark 5) for the rest of the cooking time. If stuffing is getting too brown, cover with a piece of foil. Serve hot, garnished with orange cut into eight triangular pieces. Spear on cocktail sticks and garnish joint.

---

* A long, thin jam-jar is easiest.

BACON SALAD

Serves 6

- ✦ 6 *slices cold boiled joint bacon*
- ✦ 4 *heads chicory*
- ✦ 3 *small thin-skinned oranges*
- ✦ 1½ *oz. walnut halves*
- ✦ *Maraschino cherries*
- ✦ *Juice of ½ lemon*
- ✦ *Juice of ½ orange*
- ✦ 1 *tablespoon clear honey*
- ✦ 3 *tablespoons oil*

Split heads of chicory in half, lengthwise. Cut oranges into thin slices after peeling and removing all the white pith. Arrange chicory and oranges round the edge of a flat plate and add walnut halves. Place slices of bacon in the centre and arrange cherries round the slices. Mix the fruit juices, honey and oil together and sprinkle over the salad.

SPANISH OMELETTE

- ✦ 1 *oz. butter*
- ✦ 4–6 *bacon rashers, rinded and diced*
- ✦ ½ *onion, peeled and chopped*
- ✦ 1 *large cooked potato, diced*
- ✦ 4 *large eggs*
- ✦ 4 *tablespoons milk*
- ✦ *Salt and pepper*
- ✦ 2 *heaped tablespoons cooked peas*

Melt butter in frying-pan, sauté the bacon and onion gently till onion is soft. Add potato. Beat eggs with milk and seasonings, stir in peas and pour into pan. Mix lightly and continue to cook very gently without stirring for about 5 minutes, till the omelette is nearly set and the underside golden brown. Put under a low grill to brown the top lightly and set the egg firm. Cut into slices.

HUNTINGDON FIDGET PIE

+ 1 *lb. streaky bacon diced*
+ *½ lb. onions*
+ 1 *lb. cooking apples*
+ *Seasoning*
+ *Cider*
+ 8 *oz. good short crust pastry:* (8 *oz. plain flour;*
  4 *oz. fat*)

Peel core and chop the apples roughly, also the onions. Mix these with the bacon, season well. Put in pie-dish and add cider to about half-way up dish. Cover with the pastry and bake in a moderate oven for 30 minutes at 450° F. (Gas Mark 7)—then reduce heat and cook for further 50 minutes.

YORKSHIRE PEASE PUDDING WITH BOILED BACON

Serves 4

+ 8 oz. split peas
+ Salt and pepper
+ 1 oz. butter
+ 1 egg, beaten
+ Pinch of sugar
+ 3 lb. joint forelock or collar bacon

Wash peas and soak overnight in cold water. Tie loosely in a cloth and place in a saucepan with a pinch of salt and cover with boiling water. Boil for 2½–3 hours until soft. Sieve the peas or liquidize in a blender and add the butter, egg, pepper, salt and sugar. Beat together till lightly mixed then tie up tightly in a floured cloth and boil for another 30 minutes. Serve the pease pudding with the hot bacon joint boiled for 25 minutes per pound and 25 minutes over with bayleaves, cloves and sliced onion added to the cooking liquor.

SUMMER BACON SOUP

+ 1 knuckle smoked bacon
+ 1 pig trotter
+ 1 bouquet garni
+ 10 peppercorns
+ 1 onion stuck with 4 cloves
+ 2 pints water
+ ¾ lb. mixed summer vegetables (carrots, peas, etc.)
+ 1 glass sherry

Put the knuckle, trotter and all the seasonings into a pan with the water. Bring to the boil and simmer for 1¼ hours. Strain and add the diced vegetables. Cook until tender. Add the sherry and the bacon cut from the bone. Re-season and chill thoroughly. Serve in soup cups with a slice of cucumber on top.

GLAZED APRICOT GAMMON WITH PEACHES

Serves 6–8

+ 4 *lb. joint middle gammon, boned and rolled*
+ 4 *tablespoons apricot jam*
+ *Cloves*
+ 4 *oz. demerara sugar*
+ 1 *can peach halves*

Soak bacon in cold water overnight. Place in a saucepan, cover with water and simmer for half the cooking time, allowing 25 minutes per pound and 25 minutes over. Skin the joint and place on a piece of foil. Spread the fat with apricot jam. Enclose the joint in the foil and bake at 350° F. (Gas Mark 4) for half remaining cooking time. Fold back the foil. Score the fat and stud the diamonds with cloves. Cover with brown sugar and place drained peach halves round the joint. Moisten joint with a little peach juice and bake uncovered for rest of the cooking time. Serve joint on a dish surrounded by the peaches.

COLD SLICED FOREHOCK WITH COLESLAW

Serves 6–8

- ✦ 3–4 *lb. joint forehock, boned and rolled*
- ✦ *Toasted breadcrumbs*
- ✦ 1 *small white cabbage, shredded finely*
- ✦ 1 *onion, peeled and finely chopped*
- ✦ 4 *large carrots, peeled and coarsely grated*
- ✦ 2 *oz. sultanas*
- ✦ 8 *oz. can pineapple cubes, drained*
- ✦ *Juice of ½ lemon*
- ✦ *Salt and black pepper*
- ✦ ¼–½ *pint mayonnaise*
- ✦ ½ *red pepper for garnish*

Soak joint overnight in cold water. Place in a saucepan, cover with cold water and simmer allowing 25 minutes per pound and 25 minutes over. Remove from liquor, skin and leave till cold. Mix cabbage, onion, carrots, sultanas and pineapple in a bowl. Combine mayonnaise with lemon juice and seasonings. Toss salad in mayonnaise until well coated. Slice joint and arrange on a platter with the coleslaw piled in the centre. Garnish with red pepper rings.

GINGERED COLLAR

+ 4 *lb. piece of collar bacon, rolled and tied*
+ 1 *pint ginger beer*
+ 2 *tablespoons ginger marmalade*

Soak the joint for 6 hours, if smoked, and 2 hours if unsmoked. Put into saucepan which is just big enough and add the ginger beer to cover. Bring to the boil. Reduce heat and simmer for 20 minutes further, turning occasionally in the liquid. Remove from the pan and strip skin off. Place in roasting-tin and coat the fat with the ginger marmalade. Put in a hot oven, 450° F. (Gas Mark 7), for 15 minutes until the top is glazed. Serve hot or cold.

GAMMON AND VEGETABLE RISOTTO

Serves 6

+ ½ *lb. cooked gammon, diced*
+ 3 *oz. butter*
+ 1 *large onion, peeled and chopped*
+ 1 *clove of garlic, crushed*
+ 8 *oz. long-grain rice*
+ 1¼ *pints of stock*
+ *Pinch of nutmeg*
+ *Salt and pepper*
+ 4 *heaped tablespoons cooked peas*
+ 1 *red pepper, chopped and blanched*
+ 8 *oz. can sweet corn kernels, drained*
+ 3 *oz. grated cheese*

Melt 2 oz. butter in a pan and add onion and garlic. Sauté till onion is soft but not coloured. Add rice and continue to stir for 4–5 minutes until opaque. Take saucepan off heat and add stock, nutmeg and seasonings. Bring slowly to the boil, stirring all the time. Cover and allow to simmer very gently for about 20 minutes or until all the liquid has been absorbed. Add vegetables and bacon and cook very gently for a further 5 minutes. Just before serving, mix in remaining butter and cheese.

ALMOND AND PINEAPPLE GAMMON

Serves 6–8

+ *4 lb. joint middle gammon*
+ *6 tablespoons apricot jam*
+ *3 oz. toasted split almonds*
+ *1 can pineapple rings*
+ *Stuffed olives and watercress to garnish*

Soak the bacon joint in cold water overnight. Place in a saucepan and cover with cold water. Bring to boil and simmer allowing 25 minutes per pound and 25 minutes over. Drain. Skin and allow to become quite cold. Warm and sieve the apricot jam, then spread it over outside of joint. Coat with toasted almonds. Decorate with pineapple rings dipped in apricot glaze and with olives and watercress.

WEST COUNTRY OATCAKES WITH BACON

Serves 4

+ ½ tablespoon bacon fat
+ 3 tablespoons water
+ 4 level tablespoons medium oatmeal
+ Pinch of salt
+ 4 gammon steaks, rinded and slashed
+ 4 tomatoes, halved

Melt the bacon fat with the water in a pan and sprinkle in oatmeal and salt. Work well together until smooth. Roll out the oatmeal on a board dusted with oatmeal to several cakes the size of a small saucer and very thin. Cook slowly on a pre-heated griddle or heavy frying-pan for about 10 minutes. Remove onto a tea towel in a warm place and leave to harden. Serve quickly with grilled gammon steaks and tomatoes.

TAVERN BACON

+ 3 lb. joint collar bacon
+ 1 teaspoon dry mustard
+ 2 teaspoons brown sugar
+ 4 leeks
+ 1 bayleaf
+ ½ pint ale
+ Few potato crisps

Soak the bacon for 6 hours if smoked, 2 hours if unsmoked, and then strain. Mix the sugar and dry mustard together and rub well into the joint. Place into a casserole or saucepan and add bayleaf, leeks (whole if possible) and the ale. Cover with lid and simmer either in oven at 325° F. (Gas Mark 3), or on top heat for 1½ hours. Lift joint onto a dish. Strip skin off and sprinkle with a few crushed potato crisps. Arrange leeks around the joint and serve hot. Some of the cooking liquid can be added to a rich gravy.

BACON MOUSSÉ

+ *½ lb. left-over bacon, finely chopped*
+ *4 tablespoons horse-radish sauce*
+ *2 tablespoons mayonnaise*
+ *½ teaspoon dry mustard*
+ *1 tablespoon gelatine*
+ *¼ pint cold water*
+ *¼ pint cream*

Dissolve gelatine in the cold water. Heat for 10 minutes, add to cream and mayonnaise. Beat well together and add remaining ingredients. Mix and turn into moistened mould. You can vary this to taste—unmould onto lettuce hearts and cress.

This is a good way to use left-over boiled bacon in summer to serve with salad.

LIVER AND BACON PATÉ

Serves 8–10

+ ¾ *lb. streaky bacon rashers, rinds removed*
+ 1¼ *lb. calf's or lamb's liver*
+ 6 *oz. pig's liver*
+ 1 *small onion, peeled*
+ 1 *clove garlic, crushed*
+ 1 *oz. fresh white breadcrumbs*
+ *Salt and black pepper*
+ 1 *tablespoon brandy (or sherry)*
+ 1 *egg, beaten*
+ 1 *bayleaf*

Put half the calf's or lamb's liver into a pan with water and simmer for 5 minutes. Drain and mince finely with the remaining livers, 6 oz. bacon, onion and garlic. Mix with breadcrumbs, salt, pepper, brandy (or sherry) and egg. Lay a bayleaf in the base of a loaf-tin and use all but two rashers of bacon to carefully line the tin. Fill with the liver mixture and cover with remaining bacon. Cover with a piece of greased greaseproof paper and stand in a roasting-tin containing 1 in. hot water. Cook at 350° F. (Gas Mark 4) for 1½–2 hours. Cover with a weighted plate and leave until cold before turning out.

BACON CARBONNADE

+ 1 *oz. lard*
+ 6 *oz. chopped onion*
+ 1 *crushed clove of garlic*
+ 1 *lb. shoulder bacon*
+ 2 *oz. seasoned flour*
+ 1 *can brown ale*
+ ¼ *pint water*
+ *Bouquet garni*
+ *Dash tabasco sauce*
+ *Piece lemon peel*
+ 8 *oz. button mushrooms*

Melt the lard in a flameproof casserole dish. Fry the onions and garlic for a few minutes. Cut the bacon into 1-in. squares and toss in the seasoned flour. Add this to the onions and cook for 5 minutes. Add the ale, bouquet garni, tabasco sauce, lemon peel and mushrooms. Bring to the boil. Put lid on and reduce heat. Simmer for 1¼ hours. Re-season and serve with mashed potatoes and buttered carrots.

Rice Recipes

Isuppose that when we think of rice, we naturally think of the paddy-fields of South-East Asia, or China, or of Indian restaurants. It is true that most of the rice that's eaten in the world is grown in Asia, but, of course, there is very little to spare for export. So it is that well over half the rice you buy in the shops actually comes from America.

The rice we'll be using in these recipes will be what is called long-grain rice, or Patna rice, from the days when this type was chiefly associated with that part of North-East India. It is the most common type of rice and the one usually preferred when a dish calls for savoury rice.

With rice, the most important thing, when boiling it, is to get the proportions exactly right. For every cup of rice you add two cups of water and one level teaspoon of salt. Once you've got it all in the pan, bring it to the boil, stir once, cover and leave to simmer for fifteen minutes—don't peek during this time, or it'll all go wrong. Provided you've got the proportions right, it'll work, believe me.

Another thing about rice is that it'll keep in the fridge for about a week, when cooked—but remember to cover it over, to keep in the moisture. Then, when those unexpected guests drop by it only takes a minute or so to put together our first recipe—a Gulf Coast Salad.

The Gulf Coast States of the United States of America are Texas, Louisiana and Mississippi. Florida is also on the Gulf Coast—they don't grow rice there, but the other states are the heart of America's rice-growing area.

I found this dish in the glamorous French Quarter of New Orleans—the birthplace of jazz. It's the sort of thing that would go down very well on a hot summer's day, because it's served chilled, packed with ice.

GULF COAST SALAD

Serves 4

+ *8 oz. cooked peeled prawns*
+ *6 oz. cooked long-grain rice (2 oz. rice and ¼ pint water)*
+ *3 oz. spring onions, chopped with tops*
+ *4 oz. celery, finely chopped*
+ *Salt and pepper to taste*
+ *½ teaspoon horseradish relish*
+ *½ teaspoon mustard powder*
+ *½ teaspoon chilli sauce*
+ *1 tablespoon lemon juice*
+ *6 tablespoons mayonnaise*
+ *2 tablespoons tomato sauce*

Toss prawns with rice, onion and celery. Blend remaining ingredients together and fold into the prawn and rice mixture. Chill.

Serve on lettuce leaves garnished with lemon wedges and parsley.

The next dish comes from the island of Maui—which is one of the islands in the Hawaiian group. It's called Chicken and Long-Grain Rice.

The Hawaiian Islands are a racial hotch-potch, which probably helps to explain this dish, which has its origins from all over the Pacific.

Maui itself, is the site of the earliest sugar-cane plantation on the islands, and it is still just about the only one not overrun by tourists. I found the recipe in the lovely little town of Hana, which is one of the few places you can go to and attend a traditional Luau, or party feast. You go decked with wreaths of orchids and other flowers—both men and women—and this dish is the sort of thing you may well eat.

HAWAIIAN CHICKEN AND LONG-GRAIN RICE

Serves 4

+ *3 lb. chicken, uncooked*
+ *4 tablespoons oil*
+ *1 clove garlic, chopped*
+ *1 medium-chopped onion*
+ *1½ pints chicken stock*
+ *Salt and pepper to taste*
+ *½ teaspoon powdered ginger, optional*
+ *8 oz. long-grain rice*
+ *Small can pineapple rings, drained*
+ *2 tablespoons chopped parsley*

Remove flesh from the chicken and discard skin. Use bones to make chicken stock. Cut meat into bite-size pieces. Heat oil in saucepan, add garlic, onion, sauté until onions are soft and golden (about 10 minutes). Add chicken meat, stock, salt and pepper to taste and ginger. Bring to the boil, cover and simmer for 30 minutes. Stir in long-grain rice. Simmer, covered for 15 minutes or until liquid is absorbed. To serve, turn chicken and rice into serving-dish, top with pineapple rings and sprinkle with chopped parsley.

I want to move now from Hawaii to Indonesia—which used to be called the Dutch East Indies, and even today, Indonesian cooking is very popular in Holland.

In fact, this recipe became such a favourite with the Dutch that it is now regarded as one of their traditional dishes. The last time I had it was in Amsterdam. It's called Nasi Goreng, or Indonesian Fried Rice.

Before I give you the recipe, I'd just like to tell you of a quaint old Indonesian custom. In Java, rice was thought to be the offspring of the goddess of fertility, and no Indonesian girl was considered suitable for marriage until she could make a perfect bowl of rice. Now, if you follow the simple instructions I gave you for boiling rice at the beginning of this section, ladies, you will not only have a well cooked dish of rice, you will also be eligible to get a husband!

NASI GORENG

Serves 4

✦ 2 *onions, chopped*

✦ 4 *tablespoons oil*

✦ 4 *oz. cooked meat, diced*

✦ 3 *cups cooked long-grain rice*

✦ 2 *teaspoons soy sauce or Worcester sauce*

✦ 1 *teaspoon curry powder*

✦ *Salt and pepper to taste*

✦ 2 *eggs*

✦ *Garnish: 2 tomatoes, sliced*

Fry onion in oil until tender. Add meat and cooked rice and stir until throughly mixed. Add soy sauce, curry powder, salt and pepper, stir until hot. Make a hollow in centre of rice and break eggs into it. Stir until partly scrambled, then mix with the rice, stirring until blended.

Place rice mixture onto a serving-dish and surround with sliced tomatoes.

BEEF STROGANOFF WITH PIMENTO RICE

Beef Stroganoff:

- ✦ 1½ lb. rump or fillet beef
- ✦ 2 oz. onion, finely chopped
- ✦ 4 oz. butter
- ✦ 4 oz. button mushrooms, sliced
- ✦ Salt
- ✦ A little nutmeg
- ✦ Ground black pepper
- ✦ ½ pint sour cream

Cut steak into ½ in. slices. Season to taste with freshly ground black pepper. Sauté onions in half the butter until they are lightly brown, add the sliced beef and sauté for 5 minutes, turning pieces so that all sides are brown. Remove from pan and keep warm. Add remaining butter to pan and sauté the sliced mushrooms. Return beef to pan, season to taste with salt and nutmeg. Add sour cream and heat thoroughly. Serve with Pimento Rice.

Pimento Rice

Serves 4

- ✦ 8 oz. long-grain rice
- ✦ 1 pint chicken stock
- ✦ 1 teaspoon salt
- ✦ 1 oz. butter
- ✦ 2 tablespoons chopped parsley
- ✦ 2 tablespoons diced pimento

Combine stock, rice, butter and salt. Heat to boiling, stir once, cover, reduce heat and simmer 15 minutes or until rice is tender. Add parsley and pimento. Toss lightly.

SCAMPI PROVENÇAL

Serves 4

- ✦ 8 *oz. long-grain rice*
- ✦ 1 *pint water*
- ✦ 1 *teaspoon salt*
- ✦ 2 *oz. butter*
- ✦ 1 *small onion, chopped*
- ✦ 1 *clove garlic, chopped*
- ✦ 1 *lb. frozen scampi*
- ✦ 1 *can (15 oz.) tomatoes*
- ✦ *Seasoning*
- ✦ 1 *bayleaf*

Put rice, water and salt into saucepan. Bring to boil, stir once. Cover tightly and simmer for 15 minutes. Melt butter in frying-pan, sauté onions and garlic until transparent. Add defrosted scampi and tomatoes, season to taste, add bayleaf. Continue to cook slowly for a further 5–7 minutes. Arrange cooked rice on an oval dish, make a well in centre and pour the Scampi Provençal in the middle.

CURRIED TOMATO SALAD

Serves 4

- ✦ 8 *oz. tomatoes*
- ✦ 2 *oz. butter*
- ✦ 1 *small onion, chopped*
- ✦ 1 *teaspoon curry powder*
- ✦ 1 *lb. 8 oz. cooked long-grain rice*
- ✦ 2 *tablespoons cooked peas*
- ✦ *Watercress, for garnish*

Cut the tomatoes into wedges. Melt the butter in pan and sauté the chopped onion until transparent. Add curry powder to the sautéed onion and cook for 3–4 minutes. Add the cooked rice and peas and blend thoroughly. Allow to cool. When cold add the wedges of tomatoes to the curried rice. Pile into a dish and garnish with sprigs of watercress.

SEAFOOD RICE CASSEROLE

Serves 8

- ✦ 8 *oz. long-grain rice*
- ✦ 1 *pint water*
- ✦ 1 *teaspoon salt*
- ✦ 1 *tablespoon frozen peas*
- ✦ 2 *celery stalks, chopped*
- ✦ 1 *onion, chopped*
- ✦ 8 *oz. cooked shrimps*
- ✦ 1 *can (6½ oz.) crabmeat, drained and flaked*
- ✦ ½ *pint mayonnaise*
- ✦ ¼ *pint tomato juice*
- ✦ *Salt and pepper*
- ✦ 3 *oz. blanched almonds*
- ✦ 1 *oz. butter*
- ✦ 2 *oz. grated cheddar cheese*
- ✦ *Paprika*

Put rice, water, salt into saucepan. Bring to boil, stir once. Cover tightly and simmer for 15 minutes. Stir peas, celery and onion into rice with shrimps, crabmeat, mayonnaise, tomato juice and salt and pepper to taste. Mix well and transfer to large buttered casserole. Cut almonds into shreds and fry in the butter until golden. Sprinkle on top of casserole and include butter in which nuts were fried as well. Finally top with the grated cheese and paprika. Bake just above centre of moderate oven 350° F. (Gas Mark 4) for 25 minutes.

RICE PEAR MELBA

Serves 8

+ *½ pint double cream, whipped*
+ *¾ pint rice pudding*
+ *16 pear halves, drained*
+ *¼ pint redcurrant jelly, melted*
+ *2 tablespoons Kirsch (optional)*
+ *2 oz. cashew nuts, chopped*

Fold whipped cream into left-over rice pudding, chill. Join pear halves together with a little of the rice mixture, the remainder spoon into dessert dishes and place the pears on top. Mix melted jelly with Kirsch. Spoon over fruit and sprinkle with nuts.

BEEF CURRY

Serves 4

- ✦ 1 *celery stalk*
- ✦ 2 *onions*
- ✦ 1 *clove garlic*
- ✦ 2 *tablespoons oil*
- ✦ 1 *lb. stewing steak*
- ✦ 2 *tablespoons flour*
- ✦ 1 *tablespoon curry powder*
- ✦ ¾ *pint beef stock*
- ✦ 3 *large skinned tomatoes*
- ✦ 1 *large peeled cooking apple*
- ✦ 1 *teaspoon salt*
- ✦ 2 *teaspoons sugar*
- ✦ ½ *level teaspoon powdered ginger*
- ✦ 1 *oz. desiccated coconut*
- ✦ 1 *lb. long-grain rice*
- ✦ 2 *pints water*
- ✦ *Extra desiccated coconut*

Chop celery, onion and garlic and fry in a saucepan with oil until soft. Cube steak and fry until brown. Lower heat, stir in flour and curry powder. Blend in stock. Cook, stirring until mixture boils and thickens. Simmer for 5 minutes. Chop tomato and apple and add to pan with salt, sugar, ginger and coconut. Stir well, cover pan, and simmer for 45 minutes, stirring occasionally. After 20 minutes put rice, water and salt into a saucepan. Bring to boil, stir once. Cover tightly and simmer for 15 minutes. Transfer curry to dish, sprinkle with coconut. Serve with rice.

AMERICAN RICE SALAD

Serves 4

- ✦ 12 *oz. cooked long-grain rice*
- ✦ 1 *small can pineapple, diced*
- ✦ 1 *small can peas, drained*
- ✦ 2 *tomatoes, chopped*
- ✦ 1 *dessertspoon vinegar*
- ✦ 1 *dessertspoon lemon juice*
- ✦ 2 *dessertspoons oil*
- ✦ 2 *dessertspoons single cream*
- ✦ 1 *teaspoon curry powder*
- ✦ *½ teaspoon salt*

Mix rice, pineapple, peas and tomatoes together, chill. Beat remaining ingredients thoroughly and pour over salad, toss lightly and serve on lettuce leaves.

BENGAL CURRY

Serves 6

- ✦ 1 *lb. beef steak, cubed*
- ✦ 2 *oz. butter or 2 tablespoons cooking oil*
- ✦ 12 *oz. onion, chopped*
- ✦ 2 *apples, cored and diced*
- ✦ 4 *rounds of pineapple, fresh or tinned, diced*
- ✦ 2 *tablespoons raisins*
- ✦ 2 *teaspoons salt*
- ✦ ½ *teaspoon pepper*
- ✦ 2–3 *teaspoons curry powder*
- ✦ ½ *pint beef stock*
- ✦ 1 *banana, sliced*
- ✦ *Rice for serving*
- ✦ 1 *lb. 8 oz. cooked long-grain rice*

Brown meat in butter. Add onion and curry powder, then raisins, half the apple and pineapple, seasoning and stock. Cover and simmer for 45 minutes. Add remaining fruit and simmer for 15 minutes longer. Serve over hot fluffy rice.

RICE-'N'-BEEF SALAD

Serves 4

+ 2 *large onions, sliced*
+ 1 *oz. butter*
+ 4 *oz. mushrooms, sliced*
+ 1 *large packet frozen peas, cooked*
+ 1 *lb. 8 oz. cooked long-grain rice*
+ 1 *canned pimento, sliced*
+ 12 *oz. cooked cold beef, sliced*

Fry the onion in butter until brown and crisp. Remove from the butter and drain thoroughly. Add the mushrooms to the remaining butter, cook lightly and drain. Add the onion, mushroom and peas to rice, and cool. Make a loose ring with the rice mixture around the edge of a dish, decorate with slices of pimento and serve the slices of beef in the centre.

RICE SALAD 'CEYLON'

Serves 10

- ✦ 1 *lb. long-grain rice*
- ✦ 2 *pints water*
- ✦ 2 *teaspoons salt*
- ✦ *Saffron and curry powder*
- ✦ 8 *oz. raisins*
- ✦ 2 *tablespoons brandy (optional)*
- ✦ 3 *tablespoons vinegar*
- ✦ 6 *tablespoons oil*
- ✦ ½ *teaspoon Tabasco sauce*
- ✦ 2 *tablespoons mango chutney*
- ✦ 1–2 *whole gingers, finely chopped*
- ✦ 1 *grilled chicken*
- ✦ 1 *small tin pimento, diced*
- ✦ 3 *green peppers, diced*

Put rice, water, salt, a grain of saffron and 1 dessertspoon curry powder into a large saucepan. Bring to the boil and stir once. Lower heat to simmer. Cover pan and cook about 15 minutes, without removing lid or stirring.

Marinate raisins in brandy. Make a hot sauce by combining vinegar, oil, Tabasco sauce, mango chutney and the ginger, if necessary add a little water.

Cut chicken meat into bite-size pieces, and mix into the rice together with pimento, green pepper and raisins.

Serve with the hot sauce poured over.

VEAL À LA MARSALA

Serves 4

- ✦ 8 *oz. long-grain rice*
- ✦ 1 *pint water*
- ✦ 1 *teaspoon salt*
- ✦ 2 *tablespoons olive oil*
- ✦ 8 *oz. button mushrooms*
- ✦ 6 *tablespoons chicken stock*
- ✦ *Juice ½ lemon*
- ✦ *Seasoning to taste*
- ✦ 4 *veal escalopes (4 oz. each)*
- ✦ 1 *oz. seasoned flour*
- ✦ 2 *oz. butter*
- ✦ 4 *tablespoons Marsala wine*

Put rice, water and salt into saucepan. Bring to boil, stir once. Cover tightly and simmer for 15 minutes. Heat oil in a saucepan, add mushrooms and shake for 1–2 minutes. Add stock and lemon juice, season, cover and leave on a very low heat. Beat out the 4 escalopes thinly. Sprinkle with lemon juice and coat with seasoned flour. Melt butter in a large pan, fry the veal until golden brown. Stir in the Marsala wine, cook for another 1–2 minutes. Arrange the cooked rice round the sides of a dish and place the cooked escalopes in the centre. Add the stock to the saucepan with the mushrooms, to form a sauce, cook until syrupy, pour over the veal and garnish with chopped parsley.

MUSHROOM RISOTTO

Serves 4

- ✦ 1 *lb. mushrooms, finely chopped*
- ✦ 2 *tablespoons frozen peas*
- ✦ 2 *tablespoons very finely chopped onions*
- ✦ 2 *oz. butter or margarine*
- ✦ 4 *oz. long-grain rice*
- ✦ ½ *pint chicken stock*
- ✦ ½ *teaspoon salt*

Sauté mushrooms, green peppers, and onions lightly in butter or margarine. Combine with rice, stock and salt. Place in a casserole and bake for about 40 minutes in the oven at 350° F. (Gas Mark 4). Garnish with sliced mushrooms and serve.

PEPPERY CHICKEN

Serves 4

- ✦ 3 *tablespoons cooking oil*
- ✦ 4 *chicken joints*
- ✦ 8 *very small onions, peeled*
- ✦ 1 *small green pepper, de-seeded and sliced*
- ✦ 4 *rashers streaky bacon, chopped*
- ✦ 1½ *oz. flour*
- ✦ ¾ *pint stock or water*
- ✦ 1 *teaspoon Tabasco sauce*
- ✦ *Seasoning to taste*
- ✦ 4 *oz. small mushrooms, wiped*
- ✦ 6 *oz. long-grain rice*
- ✦ ¾ *pint water*
- ✦ *Salt*

Heat the oil in a frying-pan, and fry chicken joints quickly to brown, add the onions. Remove chicken to casserole dish. Add green pepper and bacon to frying-pan, and fry for a few minutes. Transfer to casserole. Stir in the flour to the remaining oil in pan, cook for a few minutes, stirring constantly. Gradually stir in the stock, bring to the boil, stirring. Add Tabasco sauce and seasoning. Pour into the casserole, stir in mushrooms. Cover and cook in a moderate oven 350° F. (Gas Mark 4), for about 1 hour until the chicken is tender.

Put rice, water and salt into saucepan. Bring to the boil, stir once. Cover tightly and simmer for 15 minutes.

Serve chicken over rice.

VALENCIAN PAELLA

Serves 6

- ✦ 4 *tablespoons oil*
- ✦ 1 *large onion, finely chopped*
- ✦ 2 *red peppers, diced*
- ✦ 2 *green peppers, diced*
- ✦ 2 *shallots, finely chopped*
- ✦ 1 *clove garlic, finely chopped*
- ✦ 6 *oz. mushrooms, sliced*
- ✦ 8 *oz. long-grain rice*
- ✦ *Pepper and salt*
- ✦ *Saffron*
- ✦ 1 *pint chicken stock*
- ✦ 8–12 *oz. cooked chicken, diced*
- ✦ 4 *oz. cooked, peeled prawns*
- ✦ 1 *large onion, cut into rings and fried*

Heat the oil in a large pan. Gradually add onion, red and green peppers, shallots and garlic. When the vegetables are soft, add the mushrooms and heat for 1–2 minutes. Add the rice and cook for 1 minute, stirring continuously. Add pepper, salt and a grain of saffron. Add the stock gradually and bring to the boil, stir once. Cover tightly and simmer for 15 minutes. Mix in the chicken, cover and cook for a further 5 minutes. Add prawns and mix together well. Check seasoning. Turn into a casserole dish and decorate with previously fried onion rings.

GREEK LEMON SOUP

Serves 4–6

- ✦ *2 pints good chicken stock*
- ✦ *2 oz. long-grain rice*
- ✦ *2 eggs*
- ✦ *Juice of 1 lemon*
- ✦ *Seasoning to taste*

Bring stock to the boil, add rice and simmer, covered, for 15 minutes. In a basin beat the eggs and lemon juice together. Then spoonful by spoonful, and stirring continuously, add about one-third of a pint of the boiling stock to the egg mixture. Return this egg mixture to the rest of the stock and stir over *very low* heat until the soup is smooth and creamy; do not boil or the eggs will curdle. Season to taste and serve.

This may be served hot or cold.

RICE-STUFFED GREEN PEPPERS

Serves 4

- ✦ 4 *medium-sized green peppers*
- ✦ *Tomato sauce for serving*

Stuffing:
- ✦ 1 *oz. butter*
- ✦ 1 *small onion, finely chopped*
- ✦ 4 *oz. minced beef*
- ✦ 1 *teaspoon chopped parsley*
- ✦ 8 *oz. can tomatoes*
- ✦ 1 *egg*
- ✦ 6 *oz. cooked long-grain rice (2 oz. uncooked)*
- ✦ *Seasoning*

Cut peppers in half and scoop out seeds. Plunge into boiling water for 5 minutes, then drain and arrange in buttered baking-dish.

Meanwhile, prepare stuffing. Melt butter and fry onion gently until soft. Add minced beef and brown. Draw pan off heat and stir in parsley, tomatoes and egg. Add rice, season well with salt and pepper and spoon filling into pepper shells.

Place in centre of moderate oven, 350° F. (Gas Mark 4) and bake for 45 minutes. Serve with tomato sauce.

BEEF BURGUNDY

Serves 4

- ✦ 2 oz. dripping
- ✦ 1 medium-sized onion, chopped
- ✦ 2 tablespoons frozen peas
- ✦ 1½ lb. stewing steak
- ✦ Seasoned flour
- ✦ 2 tablespoons tomato purée
- ✦ 1 glass red wine
- ✦ 1 bayleaf
- ✦ ½ pint beef stock
- ✦ Seasoning to taste
- ✦ 8 oz. long-grain rice
- ✦ 1 pint of water
- ✦ 1 teaspoon salt

Melt dripping and sauté the chopped onion. Cube the stewing steak into 1½ in. cubes and mix in the seasoned flour. When onions are sautéed, add the cubed meat for 3–4 minutes, add tomato purée, peas, wine, bayleaf, stock and seasoning to taste. Allow to simmer gently for 40–45 minutes or until meat is tender. Put rice, water and salt in saucepan. Bring to boil, stir once. Cover tightly and simmer 15 minutes. Arrange the cooked rice in large dish and pour the Beef Burgundy in the centre. Garnish with a few frozen peas.

HADDOCK KEDGEREE

+ 2 *oz. butter*
+ 1 *lb. smoked cooked haddock*
+ 12 *oz. cooked long-grain rice*
+ 2 *hard-boiled eggs*
+ ¼ *pint cream*
+ *Seasoning to taste*

Melt butter in frying-pan, sauté the flaked cooked haddock for 2–3 minutes. Add the cooked rice and chopped hard-boiled eggs. Season to taste. Stir over the heat for a few minutes, shaking the pan to prevent sticking. Add ¼ pint cream and stir with a fork until the mixture has reheated and is creamy. Serve piping hot.

RICE AND FISH PORTUGUESE

+ 4 *cod cutlets or steaks*
+ 1 *large onion, chopped*
+ 1 *green pepper*
+ 4 *oz. tomatoes*
+ 1 *bayleaf*
+ *Seasoning to taste*
+ 1 *lemon*
+ 8 *oz. uncooked long-grain rice*
+ 1 *pint water*

Place the 4 cod steaks or cutlets into an ovenproof dish. Sprinkle the chopped onion over the top of the fish, together with the chopped green pepper and tomatoes. Season well and squeeze the juice of a lemon over the fish. Cut the rind of the lemon into rough pieces and place on the top of the casserole. Add the bayleaf. Cover the casserole or ovenproof dish with a lid or foil. Place in a moderate oven 350° F. (Gas Mark 4) for 30–35 minutes. During the time the fish is in the oven cook the rice in water by 1–2–1 method. Cook until light and fluffy. Arrange on an oval dish and put the Portuguese fish on top of the rice.

N.B. If you wish to cook rice in the oven, put rice in a casserole and add boiling water, cover and allow 40 minutes cooking time.

CHICKEN SOLANGE

✦ *8 oz. uncooked long-grain rice*

✦ *1 pint water*

✦ *2½ lb. chicken, cut into joints*

✦ *Butter*

✦ *1½ oz. flour*

✦ *1 tin asparagus tips*

✦ *Chicken stock*

✦ *3 tablespoons single cream*

✦ *Salt and pepper*

✦ *Tomatoes and parsley to garnish*

Brown chicken pieces in butter until tender and golden—about 20 minutes each side. Meanwhile, cook rice, fork into hot serving-dish, top with fried chicken joints. Keep warm. Stir flour into butter left in pan. Strain liquor from asparagus tips, making up to ¾ pint with chicken stock, add to the blended butter and flour, bring to boil, stirring all the time. Lower heat, add cream and asparagus, season with salt and pepper, then pour over the chicken. Garnish with tomatoes and parsley sprigs.

LOUISIANA STRAWBERRY RICE

Serves 6–8

- ✦ 4 oz. long-grain rice
- ✦ 1 pint milk
- ✦ 2 oz. sugar
- ✦ ½ teaspoon salt
- ✦ 2 oz. butter
- ✦ 1 teaspoon vanilla essence
- ✦ ½ oz. gelatine
- ✦ 2 tablespoons water
- ✦ ½ pint double cream, whipped
- ✦ 8 peach slices
- ✦ 8 whole strawberries
- ✦ 2 tablespoons Kirsch or Cointreau (optional)
- ✦ 3 oz. sugar (optional)

Combine rice, milk, sugar and salt in a saucepan, cook slowly until rice is soft and creamy, about 40–50 minutes. Stir occasionally. Blend in butter and vanilla essence. Soften gelatine in water and stir into the hot rice mixture to dissolve. Cool, but do not let it become firm. Fold in whipped cream and turn into a wet 2-pint fancy mould. Chill until well set. Marinade peaches and strawberries in Kirsch or Cointreau and 3 oz. sugar for 30 minutes. Turn out rice mould on to a cold serving-dish. Decorate with peaches and strawberries.

CHICKEN VERMOUTH WITH RICE

Serves 4

+ *4 chicken joints*
+ *2½ teaspoons salt*
+ *½ teaspoon pepper*
+ *3 medium carrots, sliced*
+ *4 oz. diced celery*
+ *3 oz. onion, thinly sliced*
+ *1 clove garlic, crushed*
+ *2 tablespoons chopped parsley*
+ *5 tablespoons dry vermouth*
+ *⅛ pint sour cream*
+ *8 oz. long-grain rice*
+ *1 pint water*
+ *1 teaspoon salt*

Sprinkle chicken joints with salt and pepper. Place next six ingredients in a 3½-pint covered casserole. Cover with double thickness of foil, place casserole lid over foil. Bake 1½ hours at 375° F. (Gas Mark 5) without removing cover. When cooked, stir in sour cream.

Put rice, water and salt in a saucepan. Bring to boil, stir once. Cover tightly and simmer for 15 minutes.

Serve chicken over rice.

SHRIMP AND RICE

Serves 6

- ✦ 6 *oz. long-grain rice*
- ✦ *¾ pint water*
- ✦ *¾ teaspoon salt*
- ✦ 8 *oz. celery, chopped*
- ✦ 4 *oz. onion, sliced*
- ✦ 2 *oz. butter*
- ✦ 12 *oz. frozen shrimps or prawns*
- ✦ 1 *small cucumber, diced*
- ✦ 2 *teaspoons salt*
- ✦ *¼ teaspoon pepper*
- ✦ 2 *tablespoons soy sauce*
- ✦ 2 *tablespoons lemon juice*

Put rice, water and salt into saucepan. Bring to boil, stir once. Cover tightly and simmer for 15 minutes.

Cook celery and onion in butter until tender. Add shrimps, cucumber, salt, pepper, soy sauce and lemon juice. Continue cooking for a few minutes until the mixture is heated.

Serve on a bed of rice.

Fresh shrimps or prawns may be used if desired. Quantity needed will be 1½ lb., these must be peeled and cooked for 5 minutes when added.

FRIED CHICKEN WITH LEMON RICE

- ✦ 4 *chicken joints*
- ✦ 8 oz. *uncooked long-grain rice*
- ✦ 1 *pint water*
- ✦ 1 *lemon grated and sliced*
- ✦ 2 *oz. butter*
- ✦ *Salt to taste*
- ✦ *Oil for frying*
- ✦ 1 *lemon quartered for garnish*

Fry chicken joints in oil, turning from time to time until lightly browned, about 10 to 15 minutes, then reduce heat, cover the pan and continue cooking for a further 15 minutes or until chicken is tender. Uncover the pan for the last 5 minutes to recrisp the skin. Meanwhile, bring water to boil, add rice, salt and slices of lemon, return to boil, stir once, lower heat to simmer, cover pan and cook about 15 minutes. Remove lemon, stir in the butter and 1 teaspoon of finely grated lemon rind. Arrange rice on a serving-dish, lay chicken joints on top and garnish with lemon quarters. Serve with a crisp salad.

ARABIAN NIGHTS PILAF

+ 2 oz. butter
+ 1 large onion, finely chopped
+ 1 crushed clove garlic (optional)
+ 8 oz. uncooked long-grain rice
+ 1 pint chicken stock
+ 8 oz. cooked poultry, diced
+ 2 tablespoons raisins
+ Salt and pepper
+ 1 oz. chopped salted almonds, peanuts or walnuts
+ 8 bacon rolls
+ 8 cocktail sausages

Melt half the butter and fry the onion and garlic very gently until soft but not browned. Add the rice, stir and fry for several minutes. Add the stock, bring to the boil, cover and simmer for about 15 minutes, until the rice is cooked and liquid absorbed. Add the poultry, raisins, remaining 1 oz. butter and seasoning to taste; stir well and keep warm while grilling the bacon rolls and cocktail sausages. To serve, pile the pilaf on an oval dish, sprinkle the nuts on top and surround with alternate bacon rolls and sausages.

BEEF AND CAULIFLOWER ON RICE

Serves 6

+ 1 *lb. beef steak (stewing steak will do)*
+ 1 *small head of cauliflower*
+ 2 *oz. butter or margarine*
+ 1 *green pepper, cut in ¾ in. squares*
+ 1 *clove garlic, crushed*
+ 4 *tablespoons soy sauce*
+ 1 *tablespoon cornflour*
+ 4 *tablespoons water*
+ ½ *teaspoon sugar*
+ 3 *oz. sliced onion*
+ 1 *lb. 2 oz. hot cooked long-grain rice*

Cut meat into ½ in. squares. Separate cauliflower into flower-ettes. Brown meat in butter for about 1 minute. Remove meat from pan and keep warm. Add cauliflower, green pepper, soy sauce and garlic. Toss lightly with a fork until vegetables are coated with soy sauce. Cover pan tightly and simmer until veg-etables are barely tender, about 10 minutes. Blend cornflour, water and sugar. Add to vegetables, with meat and onions. Cook, stirring constantly, until thoroughly heated and sauce thickened. Serve over hot cooked rice.

SOLE ELEGANTE WITH FLUFFY RICE

Serves 6

- ✦ 6 *fillets (1½ lb.) sole or plaice*
- ✦ 2 *oz. onions, chopped*
- ✦ 1 *oz. butter or margarine*
- ✦ ¼ *pint salad dressing*
- ✦ 1 *(10½ oz.) can cream of mushroom soup*
- ✦ 1 *teaspoon salt*
- ✦ ¼ *teaspoon pepper*
- ✦ 2 *oz. canned pimento, diced*
- ✦ 1 *lb. 2 oz. hot cooked long-grain rice (6 oz. rice and ¾ pint water and salt)*

Roll up fillets. Place with cut end down in a shallow casserole. Sauté onion in butter until tender but not brown. Blend in salad dressing and soup. Add salt and pepper. Cook until smooth, stirring constantly. Spoon over fish. Sprinkle with pimento. Bake at 350° F. (Gas Mark 4) for 25 minutes or until fish flakes easily.

To serve: Spoon hot cooked rice onto a heated plate. Place fish on top of rice, spoon sauce over fish.

CROWN PORK CHOPS WITH ORANGE PEEL

Serves 6

- ✦ *2 joints of 6 pork cutlets*
- ✦ *Salt and pepper*
- ✦ *2 oz. butter*
- ✦ *8 oz. celery, grated*
- ✦ *6 oz. onion, chopped*
- ✦ *1 lb. long-grain rice*
- ✦ *1 teaspoon salt*
- ✦ *1½ pints chicken stock*
- ✦ *½ pint orange juice*
- ✦ *4 oz. raisins*
- ✦ *1 dessertspoon grated orange peel*

Ask the butcher to partially chop the cutlets. Form them into a circle and sew the two joints together. Season with salt and pepper. Roast the meat (45 minutes per pound) and baste frequently with the juice of the meat. To make orange rice, melt butter in a saucepan, add celery and onion, then add rice and salt. Pour chicken stock and orange juice over the mixture. Bring to boil, stir once. Cover tightly and simmer for 15 minutes. Five minutes before serving, mix in raisins and orange peel. Serve the crown of pork filled with orange rice.

COQ AU VIN

Serves 6

- ✦ *8 oz. pork belly*
- ✦ *8 oz. onion, chopped*
- ✦ *6 chicken joints*
- ✦ *8 oz. mushrooms, sliced*
- ✦ *Garlic salt*
- ✦ *Chopped parsley*
- ✦ *Thyme*
- ✦ *¾ pint red wine*
- ✦ *12 oz. long-grain rice*
- ✦ *1½ pints water*
- ✦ *1½ teaspoons salt*
- ✦ *1 tablespoon cornflour*
- ✦ *2 tablespoons brandy*

Cut the pork into cubes, add chopped onion and cook in its own fat for 15 minutes, until half cooked. Add chicken joints and mushrooms. Flavour with garlic salt, parsley and thyme, add red wine. Simmer slowly until cooked. Put rice, water and salt into saucepan. Bring to the boil, stir once. Cover tightly and simmer for 15 minutes. Before serving, mix the cornflour with a little water and stir into the chicken mixture to thicken. Flavour with brandy.

Serve over hot cooked rice.

BASIC METHODS OF COOKING RICE

Proportions = 1 cup long-grain rice + 2 cups water + 1 level teaspoon salt.

Oven Method:
Put rice and salt into an ovenproof casserole, add boiling water and stir (using the same proportions as above). Cover with lid and cook in a moderate oven 350° F. (Gas Mark, 4) for about 40 minutes. Test rice, and if not quite tender, or water not absorbed completely, cover and cook for another few minutes. Fluff rice lightly with fork and serve.

Fried Rice:
Melt 1 oz. butter in a large saucepan. And 1 finely chopped onion and stir in the cup of rice. Fry over moderate heat, stirring well until rice is golden brown. Add 2 cups of boiling water and 1 teaspoon salt. Bring to boil, stir once, cover tightly and simmer for 15 minutes.

Buttered Rice:
Add a thick slice of lemon while the rice is cooking. Just before serving remove lemon and fork 1–2 oz. butter into the dry fluffy rice.

Herb Rice:
Prepare as for buttered rice but add 1 heaped tablespoon each of fresh parsley and either chives or spring onion, all finely chopped.

Golden Rice:
To every 8 oz. rice add ⅛ teaspoon of powdered saffron. When dry and fluffy, fork in 1 oz. butter and 2 oz. coarsely chopped toasted walnuts or almonds.

Curried Rice:
Fry 1 tablespoon of finely chopped onion in 1 oz. butter. When soft, stir in 1 dessertspoon curry powder. Add water and rice, when water is absorbed and rice fluffy, fork in 1 oz. butter.

Cream, Milk, and Yogurt Recipes

Ihave a secret that I want to let you in on—in Georgia, which is now part of Russia, and in parts of Turkey, the men live to a great age, and can father children when well past 100 years of age.

The secret, so they tell me, is their daily intake of yogurt! There is an old Turkish saying: 'Eat yogurt every day for 100 years and you will live to be 100.'

I have a young daughter myself, she's a wonderful person called Mary Victoria, whom I adore, but what any person—Turk or not—would want with a baby when they're past 100 really defeats me. However here, for what it's worth, I am including the genuine Turkish recipe for making yogurt eating more enjoyable.

TURKISH YOGURT FLUFF

Serves 4

+ 1 *tin mandarin oranges*
+ 1 *carton yogurt*
+ 2 *tablespoons double dairy cream*
+ 1 *oz. sugar (optional)*
+ 2 *egg-whites*

Strain juice from oranges. Roughly chop mandarin oranges and mix together with cream, yogurt and sugar if required. Whisk up egg-whites stiffly and fold into yogurt mixture. Serve chilled, and decorate with whole mandarin segments and whipped double cream. Different varieties of fruit and flavours of yogurt can be used.

Cream is much too rarely used in cooking—one-third of the British, so the Board of Trade informs me—never buy or use cream in any form, not even in their coffee.

This is not so in other parts of the world, especially in those countries where cream is cheaper and the economy more rural. It's a great treat to land in, say Switzerland, and find cream added to the cookery as a matter of course, rather than as a once-a-year treat.

The recipes I've selected for you I hope will encourage you to make use of cream, at least in small amounts. Anyhow, if economy is the problem, there are many more things I'd rather cut down on before I gave up using cream in my cookery.

My first cream recipe I call an American Ice-Box Cake. This is the name it goes by in New York, though I believe it originally came from Italy. It's a perfect example of how to make a really luxurious sweet, the only thing you have to worry about with it is how much of it your diet will allow you to eat, because it really is very, very rich.

AMERICAN ICE-BOX CAKE

Serves 8

- ✦ *Eggs*
- ✦ *Salt*
- ✦ *Sugar*
- ✦ *Cream*
- ✦ *Plain chocolate*
- ✦ *Strawberries*

Meringue Layers:

Preheat oven to very slow. Electric 250° F. (Gas Mark ½). Beat together 4 egg-whites, 7 oz. caster sugar and a pinch of salt until stiff and glossy. Line baking-sheets with aluminium foil or waxed paper and on the paper trace three circles, each 8 in. in diameter. Spread the meringue evenly over the circles, about ¼ in. thick and bake in the very slow oven for about 1½ hours until meringue is pale gold but still pliable. Remove from oven and carefully peel waxed paper from bottom. Put on cake racks to dry.

Filling:

Melt over hot water 6 oz. plain chocolate. Whip ½ pint double cream until stiff with 1 oz. caster sugar. Slice half a pound of strawberries.

Presentation:

Place a meringue layer on serving-plate and spread with a thin coating of melted chocolate. Then spread a layer about ¾ in. thick of the whipped cream and top this with a layer of sliced strawberries. Put a second layer of meringue on top, spread with chocolate, another layer of the whipped cream and sliced strawberries, then top with third layer of meringue. Decorate top meringue layer in an informal pattern using whole ripe strawberries and piped cream. Refrigerate for 2 hours before serving.

My next recipe is hot off the press, as it were, because I cooked it for the first time in this form for the TV series, and being a very gallant man I named it after one of the producers. 'Soufflé Pudding Charmian' is a cross between a soufflé and a custard pudding served with a delicious fresh peach sauce. It is easy to prepare, and makes a light, tasty dessert for any meal.

SOUFFLÉ PUDDING CHARMIAN

Serves 6

- ✦ *1 oz. flour*
- ✦ *1½ oz. butter*
- ✦ *1½ oz. sugar*
- ✦ *Milk*
- ✦ *Sherry (optional)*
- ✦ *Lemons*
- ✦ *Salt*
- ✦ *Eggs*
- ✦ *Peaches*
- ✦ *Redcurrant jelly*

Soufflé Pudding:

Preheat the oven to moderately hot, 370° F. (Gas Mark 4). Heat in a saucepan ½ pint milk with a pinch of salt. Cream together 1 oz. flour, 1½ oz. butter and 1½ oz. sugar. When the milk boils, add this mixture and stir well for ½ minute. Remove from fire and cool slightly. Separate 3 eggs. Add the yolks to the mixture in saucepan. Mix well. Add the grated rind of 1 lemon. Beat the egg-whites until firm. Add them to mixture gently with a spoon. Put in 2¼ pint soufflé dish which has been greased and sugared in the moderately hot oven for about 30 minutes.

Sauce:

In a saucepan melt 3 fl. oz. of redcurrant jelly and 2 fl. oz. of sherry (optional). Add to the warm liquid: ¼ lb. sliced peaches and a squeeze of lemon juice.

Presentation:

Serve with hot peach sauce.

APRICOT AND PEAR RICE RING
WITH SAUCE

Serves 6–8

✦ 2 tablespoons gelatine powder

✦ 6 oz. long-grain rice

✦ 2 pints milk

✦ 5 oz. granulated sugar

✦ 1 teaspoon vanilla essence

✦ ¼ pint single dairy cream

Centre Filling:

✦ 1 (16 oz.) tin apricots

✦ 2 ripe dessert pears, sliced, cored and dipped in lemon juice

Sauce:

✦ ½ lb. dried apricots, soaked for 24 hours in just enough water to cover

✦ ½ lb. cooking apples, peeled, cored and chopped

✦ Sugar to taste

✦ ¼–½ teaspoon almond essence

✦ Apricot brandy to taste, if desired

Stir the powdered gelatine into 8 fl. oz. of cold water and leave to soften. In the top of a double saucepan, cook the long-grain rice with the milk, over boiling water for 15 minutes. Stir in the sugar and vanilla essence, then stir every 15 minutes for about 45 minutes or until the rice is just tender. Remove from the heat and stir in the softened gelatine until dissolved. Transfer the rice mixture to a chilled bowl and leave in cold water to cool but not set. Fold in the cream, mix well and pour into a wetted 2¼–2½

116

pint ring mould, and leave for approximately 4 hours in a cold place to set. Dip the mould in hot water and unmould. Fill the centre with the apricots and pear slices.

To make the sauce, cook the apricots in the water, with the chopped apples. Bring to the boil and simmer, covered for 1 hour stirring occasionally. Stir in enough sugar to taste, the almond essence, and apricot brandy, if desired. Pass through a sieve. Chill. Spoon the sauce over the fruit and around the bottom edge of the mould. Any remaining sauce should be served separately.

FLORENTINE PANCAKES

Serves 4

Pancake Batter:
+ *4 oz. flour*
+ *Pinch salt*
+ *1 standard egg*
+ *½ pint milk*
+ *Oil or lard for frying*

Filling:
+ *2 large onions, finely chopped*
+ *½ oz. butter*
+ *2 oz. streaky bacon, cut into strips*
+ *1 large packed (14 oz.) frozen chopped spinach*

Sauce:
+ *1 oz. butter*
+ *1 oz. flour*
+ *¼ pint milk*
+ *2 tablespoons real dairy cream*
+ *Salt and pepper*

For the Batter:
Sift flour and salt into a bowl, make well in the centre and drop egg into it. With a wooden spoon gradually work in flour and egg with half the milk. Beat well until smooth then beat in remaining milk. Pour into a jug. Heat a little oil or lard in a 7 in. frying-pan. Pour in enough batter to *thinly* coat base of pan. Cook until underside is golden brown then turn and cook on other side. Place on a plate and keep warm. Make 8 pancakes with the batter.

For the Filling:

Lightly fry onion and bacon in butter in a saucepan for 4–5 minutes. Add frozen spinach and cover with a tight-fitting lid. *Leave* for 5 minutes on a high heat. Remove lid, stir and for 4 minutes stir occasionally until really dry in consistency.

(*Note:* It begins to hiss loudly only when it's dry enough.)

For the Sauce:

Melt butter, stir in flour and cook for 2 minutes. Remove from heat and gradually add milk. Return to heat, bring to the boil and cook for 2 minutes, stirring continuously. Stir in the spinach mixture, season to taste and add 2 tablespoons of cream.

To serve, place filling along centre of each pancake and roll up.

Note: This dish makes a good starter, in which case the above quantities would serve 8 people.

CHOCOLATE HAZELNUT GATEAU

+ 8 *oz. caster sugar*
+ 1 *rounded dessertspoon cocoa*
+ 4 *egg-whites*
+ 2 *oz. hazelnuts*
+ ½ *pint double dairy cream*

Mark circles 7 in. in diameter onto three pieces of greaseproof paper on three baking-sheets. Oil thoroughly, sieve the sugar and cocoa together. Whisk the egg-whites until stiff. Whisk in half the sugar and cocoa. Gradually fold in the remaining half. Using a ½ in. nozzle pipe spread the meringue on the marked circles. Cook in a slow oven 225° F. (Gas Mark ½) for approximately 2–3 hours or until meringues dry throughout. Carefully remove from paper and turn onto a cooling tray.

Chop the hazelnuts, keeping back a few for decoration. Whip the cream until stiff. Sandwich layers of meringue together with cream and chopped nuts. Spread cream on the top and decorate with whole nuts and grated chocolate.

MANDARIN CREAM CRUNCH

Serves 6

+ *6 oz. butter*
+ *8 oz. white breadcrumbs*
+ *2 oz. soft brown sugar*
+ *1 (11-oz.) can mandarin oranges, drained*
+ *¼ pint mandarin juice*
+ *2 level teaspoons cornflour*
+ *A few drops of orange colouring*
+ *½ pint double dairy cream, lightly whipped*

Melt butter in a large frying-pan. Add breadcrumbs and fry gently until golden brown and crisp. Allow to cool and stir in sugar. Reserve a few mandarin oranges for decoration. Blend cornflour with mandarin juice and heat until thickened. Add a few drops of orange colouring. Mix with remaining mandarin oranges and allow to cool. Spoon half the mandarin orange mixture into base of a glass serving-bowl. Cover with half the whipped cream, and then half the breadcrumbs. Repeat each layer once more, reserving a small amount of cream for decoration. Decorate the top with the remaining mandarin oranges and whipped cream.

APPLE AND CITRUS SOUFFLÉ

Serves 6–8

+ 1 *pint apple purée*
+ *Juice of* 2 *large oranges*
+ ¼ *pint single dairy cream*
+ ¾ *oz. gelatine dissolved in* 2 *tablespoons water*
+ ¼ *pint double dairy cream, whipped*
+ 3 *egg-whites, stiffly beaten*
+ 2 *oz. toasted coconut*
+ 2 *red-skinned apples, cored and sliced*
+ *Juice of* 1 *lemon*
+ 2 *oz. glacé cherries (chopped)*

Combine the apple purée, orange juice, single cream and dissolved gelatine. When on the point of setting fold in the whipped
cream and then the stiffly beaten egg-whites. Pour into a 6–7
in. soufflé dish, bound with a deep band of greaseproof paper.
Refrigerate to set. Carefully remove greaseproof band, and coat
sides of soufflé with toasted coconut. Decorate with apple slices,
dipped in lemon juice, and chopped glacé cherries.

PINEAPPLE CUSTARD PUDDING

+ 4 *stale sponge cakes*
+ 1 *pint milk*
+ 3 *eggs*
+ 3 *oz. caster sugar*
+ ¼ *teaspoon almond flavouring*
+ 2 *pineapple rings drained from juice, dried on a cloth and finely chopped*
+ *Real dairy cream*

Crush stale cakes to fine crumbs, beat eggs and sugar until creamy and well blended, gradually stir in the milk, then the crumbs, pineapple and flavouring. Stand the pie-dish in a tin containing about 1 in. of water and bake at 275° F. (Gas Mark 2) for approximately 2 hours or until the top of the custard feels firm and a knife inserted in the centre of the pudding comes out cleanly. Put away to become ice cold. Pipe round the edge of the custard with real dairy cream, cover the top of the pudding inside the piped ring, with neatly arranged wedges of pineapple drained, dried and cut from the rings. If liked, the rings may be cut right through using a sharp knife to make two thinner rings, then the wedges may be arranged overlapping like tiles with a very attractive effect.

Cream:

Whip ¼ pint double cream with 1 level tablespoon of icing sugar and 1 tablespoon of pineapple juice.

ORANGE ROSE CREAMS

Serves 4

+ 2 *almond macaroons*
+ *½ can mandarin oranges*
+ 1 *egg-white*
+ 1 *level dessertspoon caster sugar*
+ *¼ pint double dairy cream*
+ 1 *tablespoon milk*
+ 3 *dessertspoons orange juice and rose-hip syrup*
+ *Green leaves for decoration*

Break up macaroons and put into four sundae glasses. Top with equal amounts of mandarin oranges and syrup from the can. Beat egg-white to a stiff snow. Add sugar and continue beating until mixture is shiny and stands in high firm peaks. Whip cream and milk together until thick. Stir in orange juice and rose-hip syrup. Fold cream mixture into beaten egg-white. Pile into glasses over macaroons and fruit. Chill thoroughly. Eat within 4 hours of making.

Just before serving, decorate with fresh leaves—lemon balm or mint.

RASPBERRY CREAM PANCAKES

Cream Pancakes:

+ *4 oz. flour*
+ *Large pinch salt*
+ *1 standard egg*
+ *¼ pint single cream*
+ *¼ pint milk*

Topping:

+ *1 tablespoon water*
+ *½ lb. raspberries*
+ *1 oz. caster sugar*
+ *¼ pint double dairy cream, lightly whipped*

To Make Pancakes:

Sift flour and salt into bowl. Add egg and cream. Beat well until mixture is smooth. Add milk. Lightly grease frying-pan and heat until fat is hot. Pour in single tablespoons of batter to make pancakes of about 3 in. in diameter. Cook until the underside of the pancake is golden. Turn or toss pancake and cook until second side is golden. Turn out of pan and keep warm. Use rest of batter to make pancakes in this way. For each serving, arrange 6 pancakes on a plate.

To Make Raspberry Topping:

Put water with raspberries in a pan, sprinkle over sugar and heat gently until sugar dissolves and the mixture is piping hot.

Top pancakes with a circle of raspberries and a large spoonful of whipped cream. If liked, sprinkle caster sugar and serve with real dairy cream.

CHOCOLATE RUM

+ 1 *cup hot milk*
+ 2 *teaspoons drinking chocolate*
+ 3 *teaspoons rum*

Pour the hot milk into a cup. Quickly stir in the drinking chocolate and rum. Serve at once.

RASPBERRY CHOCOLATE BLISS

Serves 4

+ 1 (15 *oz.*) *can raspberries*
+ 6 *oz. fresh brown breadcrumbs*
+ 6 *oz. caster sugar*
+ 1½ *oz. plain chocolate, grated*
+ ¼ *pint double dairy cream*
+ ¼ *pint single dairy cream*
+ 1 *tablespoon sherry*

Drain the raspberries and divide between four individual dishes reserving a few for decoration. Mix together breadcrumbs, sugar and 1¼ oz. of the chocolate. Whip the creams together and stir in the sherry. Layer the breadcrumbs. Place remaining cream in a piping bag with a large star nozzle attached and pipe a whirl of cream in the centre of each dish. Decorate with raspberries and sprinkle with the remaining chocolate.

Note: Juice from raspberries may be used for making a jelly.

PINEAPPLE CHOCOLATE RING

- ✦ 1 *pineapple jelly*
- ✦ *½ pint hot water*
- ✦ 3 *tablespoons sugar*
- ✦ *½ pint milk*
- ✦ 1 *tablespoon cocoa*
- ✦ 1 *small tin pineapple rings or pieces*
- ✦ *Fresh whipped cream*

Make the jelly using the hot water. Blend the cocoa and sugar with a little of the milk. Heat the remaining milk. Add to the blended mixture. Return to the saucepan and boil for one minute. When both mixtures are cool whisk together. Pour into a mould and stand in a cold place to set. Turn on to a serving-dish, fill the centre with fresh whipped cream and decorate with pineapple, cherry and angelica.

RHUBARB PAVLOVA CAKE

Serves 6

+ 4 *egg-whites*
+ 8 *oz. caster sugar*
+ ½ *teaspoon vanilla essence*
+ ½ *teaspoon cornflour*
+ ½ *teaspoon vinegar*
+ ½ *oz. flaked almonds*

Filling:
+ 1 *lb. early rhubarb*
+ 1 *tablespoon water*
+ 4 *oz. caster sugar*
+ ½ *pint double dairy cream, whipped*
+ 1 *tablespoon Kirsch (optional)*

Whisk the egg-whites until stiff and peaky. Beat in sugar, teaspoon by teaspoon, until all has been incorporated. Fold in vanilla essence, cornflour and vinegar. Spread a 7 in. circle of meringue on one end of greased greaseproof paper or foil standing on a baking-sheet, making the sides higher than the centre to form a shell to hold the filling: For the top spoon 2 tablespoons meringue on the greased greaseproof paper. Dust with caster sugar and sprinkle with flaked almonds. Dry out at 200° F. (Gas Mark ¼) for about 4–5 hours until firm but still white.

Filling:

Cut rhubarb into 1 in. lengths and stew gently in water with sugar, in a tightly lidded pan. Cool. Gently fold in whipped cream and Kirsch keeping the rhubarb whole. Turn into meringue case and top with meringue circle and serve.

CREAMY APPLE CRUNCH

+ 6 *oz. digestive biscuits*
+ 3 *oz. melted butter*
+ 3 *oz. soft brown sugar*
+ 1 *level tablespoon cocoa*
+ 2 *lb. cooking apples*
+ ½ *pint water*
+ 4 *oz. granulated sugar*
+ ½ *oz. (1 envelope) gelatin*
+ 4 *tablespoons water*
+ *A little green colouring (optional)*
+ ½ *pint double dairy cream*
+ *Chocolate for decoration*

Crush the digestive biscuits finely, add melted butter, brown sugar and cocoa. Combine well then press firmly into a loose-bottomed 7 in. cake-tin.

Peel, core and slice the apples, put in a saucepan with ½ pint water and granulated sugar. Cook gently until apples are very soft and pulpy. Beat well. Soak gelatine in the 4 tablespoons water, then add softened gelatine and a little green colouring if desired. Cool, when just on the point of setting, whip cream until stiff and fold into apple. Turn into cake-tin on top of biscuit crust. Chill. Push bottom of cake-tin up, then slide cake into a plate. Decorate with chocolate curls.

APPLE AND MINCEMEAT SYLLABUB

Serves 8–10

+ ¾ *pint apple purée*
+ ½ *lb. mincemeat*

Syllabub:

+ *Pared rind and juice of* 1 *lemon marinaded overnight in 4 fl. oz. white wine or sherry and 2 tablespoons brandy*
+ *2 oz. sugar*
+ *½ pint double dairy cream*
+ *2 red-skinned apples, chopped*
+ *Lemon juice*

Mix the apple purée with the mincemeat and put one table-spoon of the mixture in the base of each glass. When the rind and lemon juice have marinaded in the wine and brandy overnight, strain the liquid into a large, deep bowl. Add the sugar and stir until dissolved. Pour the cream in slowly, stirring all the time. Add a little grated nutmeg and whisk until just thickened. Spoon the syllabub into glasses and top lightly with a spoonful of the remaining apple and mincemeat mixture. Decorate with chopped apple, sprinkle with lemon juice (to prevent discolouring). Keep in a cool place until ready to serve.

VARIOUS MILK SHAKES

SPICED MILK SHAKE

For 1 Portion:
- ✦ *2 tablespoons spiced syrup*
- ✦ *¼ pint milk*
- ✦ *1 brickette dairy ice-cream*
- ✦ *Ground cinnamon (optional)*

Whisk the syrup, milk and ice-cream together until well blended and frothy. Pour into a tall glass and sprinkle a little ground cinnamon on top. Serve with a straw.

Syrup:
- ✦ *3 oz. sugar*
- ✦ *½ level teaspoon cinnamon*
- ✦ *¼ pint water*
- ✦ *4 cloves*
- ✦ *2 teaspoons lemon juice*

Blend the cinnamon with the sugar then add the water, cloves and lemon juice. Bring slowly to the boil, stirring all the time. Simmer gently for 5 minutes. Strain and leave to cool. Store in an airtight jar and use as required.

SPANISH FROSTEE

Serves 4

- ✦ 2 *oranges*
- ✦ 1 *pint milk*
- ✦ 3–4 *tablespoons Curaçao or Cointreau*
- ✦ 4 *brickettes of dairy ice-cream*

Cut half of one of the oranges into slices and set aside for decoration. Squeeze the juice from the remaining 1½ oranges. Pour the milk into a basin. Add the orange juice, liqueur and half the ice-cream cut into cubes. Whisk the mixture until well blended and frothy. Pour into glasses, top with small piece of ice-cream and decorate each glass with a slice of orange. Serve at once.

ICED STRAWBERRY CRUSH
(For One)

- ✦ ¼ *pint milk*
- ✦ 4 *tablespoons sieved strawberries*
- ✦ 1 *brickette dairy ice-cream*
- ✦ *A whole strawberry for decoration*

Place the milk and sieved strawberries into a screw-top jar, add the ice-cream cut into pieces. Cover the jar securely and shake vigorously for about 2 minutes. Pour into a glass, spear a whole strawberry with a cocktail stick and balance over the top of glass. Serve at once.

WIMBLEDON WHIP

+ 4 *level tablespoons lemon curd*
+ 1 *pint milk*
+ 12 *tablespoons water*
+ 4 *brickettes dairy ice-cream*
+ 8 *teaspoons lemon juice*
+ *Slices of cucumber and sprigs of mint to garnish*

Stir the lemon curd and water together until well blended, then add lemon juice. Pour the milk in a basin and gradually stir in the lemon mixture.

Finally, add the ice-cream, cut into cubes, and whisk vigorously until frothy. Pour into tall glasses and serve immediately, garnished with the cucumber and mint.

SAVOURY MILK AND CREAM DISHES

CREAMY KIPPER SCALLOPS

Serves 4

Filling:

+ 1 *lb. kipper fillets or* 1 (10 *oz.*) *packet of boil-in-the-bag kipped fillets, uncooked*
+ 1½ *oz. butter*
+ 1½ *oz. flour*
+ ¾ *pint milk*
+ 1 *lemon, finely grated rind*

Topping;

+ ¾ *lb. potatoes, peeled*
+ ¾ *oz. butter*
+ 2 *tablespoons milk*
+ 1½ *oz. breadcrumbs*
+ *Parsley for garnish*

Put potatoes on to boil. Cut kipper fillets into ½ in. cubes; divide equally between four large scallop shells. Melt butter for filling, stir in flour and cook for 2–3 minutes without browning. Remove from heat, gradually stir in milk, return to heat and bring to boil. Cook 3–4 minutes and stir in lemon rind. Divide equally over the kipper pieces.

Mash and cream potatoes with butter and milk. Fit a large forcing bag with a star pipe and fill the bag with the creamed potato. Pipe rosettes round outside of shells. Sprinkle breadcrumbs on centre part of each scallop. Place scallops on baking-sheet and bake in moderate oven, 375° F. (Gas Mark 5) for 20–25 minutes until a delicate golden brown. Garnish with sprigs of parsley and serve hot.

CREAMY HERRING ROE QUICHE

Serves 4

For Pastry:

+ 6 *oz. plain flour*
+ 1 *teaspoon salt*
+ 3 *oz. butter*
+ 3 *tablespoons water*

For Filling:

+ ½ *oz. butter*
+ 1 *small onion*
+ 2 *eggs*
+ ¼ *pint double dairy cream*
+ 8 *oz. can soft herring roes*
+ *Salt and pepper to taste*
+ 2 *tomatoes, skinned and sliced*
+ 1 *extra tomato for garnish*

To Make Pastry:

Sift flour and salt. Rub in butter until mixture resembles fine breadcrumbs. Add water to bind into stiff dough. Knead lightly and leave to rest in cool place for 10 minutes. Roll out pastry and use to line 8 in. flan ring on baking-tray. Line with foil and beans and bake 'blind' in hot oven, 425° F. (Gas Mark 7) for 15 minutes. Remove foil and beans and continue baking 5 minutes until pastry is cooked.

To Make Filling:

Melt butter in saucepan. Chop onions finely and cook gently in butter 4–5 minutes, without browning. Allow to cool. Place eggs and cream in large bowl and beat thoroughly. Add soft roes, salt and pepper; mix well, slightly breaking up the roes.

Place chopped onion into base of flan-case, top with sliced tomatoes and seasoning. Pour over egg mixture. Bake in moderate oven, 375° F. (Gas Mark 5) for 40–45 minutes, until mixture is set. Garnish with extra slices of tomato and serve with a salad.

NEW YEAR VOL-AU-VENT

Serves 4–6

+ *9 oz. puff pastry*
+ *1 egg, beaten*

Filling:

+ *3 oz. butter*
+ *2 oz. flour*
+ *1 pint milk*
+ *Salt*
+ *Pepper*
+ *Pinch cayenne*
+ *1 medium-sized onion, finely chopped*
+ *2 oz. mushrooms, thickly sliced*
+ *6 rashers streaky bacon, chopped*
+ *1 lb. cooked turkey, roughly chopped*
+ *2 oz. raisins*
+ *2 oz. peanuts*

Garnish:

+ *4 cooked bacon rolls*
+ *Sprigs of parsley*

Roll out pastry to a 9 in. square, about ¼ in. thick, and trim edges. Place on a baking-tray. Mark a square 1½ in. from edge and cut half-way through pastry. Glaze with beaten egg. Bake at 450° F. (Gas Mark 8) for 20 minutes.

Filling:

Make a white sauce by melting 2 oz. of the butter in a pan, add flour and cook for 1 minute. Remove from heat and gradually blend in milk. Return to heat, cook until thickened, stirring all the time. Season to taste. Melt remaining 1 oz. butter in a pan and gently fry onion for 1 minute. Add chopped bacon and mushrooms and cook for a further 2–3 minutes. Add cooked turkey, peanuts and raisins. Mix into white sauce. Reheat and adjust seasoning.

To Serve:

Cut out marked square from vol-au-vent to use as a lid. Place turkey filling in middle of vol-au-vent, replace lid and garnish with cooked bacon rolls. Reheat if necessary before serving. Garnish finally with parsley sprigs.

GARNISHED MILK CHICKEN

- ✦ *2 small spring chickens*
- ✦ *1 small onion stuck with 2 cloves*
- ✦ *2 small under-ripe bananas*
- ✦ *1 level dessertspoonful flour*
- ✦ *1 pint milk*
- ✦ *3 eggs*
- ✦ *Green peas*
- ✦ *Salt, pepper*

Cover the chickens with warm water in a saucepan, season with salt, bring to the boil, remove any scum, replace lid and cook gently for 35 minutes. Drain off the liquid (use for soup) and pour in the milk and add the onion. Simmer gently for 30 minutes. Take up the birds and keep them hot. Thicken the milk with the flour, then stir in one of the eggs, beaten, cook and stir over a gentle heat until very smooth and creamy, season to taste with pepper and salt. Pour a little of the sauce over the birds, garnish with slices of the remaining eggs, ready hard-boiled, and rings of banana very thinly sliced. Arrange peas round the birds, hand the rest of the sauce separately.

SAVOURY FESTIVE PIE

Serves 4–6

+ *2 oz. butter*
+ *1 onion, peeled and chopped*
+ *2 oz. mushrooms, washed and sliced*
+ *2 oz. flour*
+ *1 pint milk*
+ *8 oz. cooked turkey or chicken (boned and chopped)*
+ *8 oz. cooked ham (chopped)*
+ *A little lemon juice*
+ *Salt and pepper*
+ *1 large packet instant potato*

+ *An ovenproof dish, greased, with a liquid capacity of at least 2 pints*

Heat the butter in a pan and fry the onion and mushrooms gently until lightly browned. Stir in the flour and cook for a few minutes without browning. Remove pan from the heat and gradually add the milk. Return to the heat and bring to the boil, stirring continuously. Add chicken and ham, lemon juice and seasoning to taste. Place mixture in prepared dish. Make up the instant potato as directed on the packet. Add a knob of butter, then place the potato in a large piping bag with a star nozzle attached. Pipe a rope design all over the surface of the pie. Alternatively, the potato may be forked. Bake in a fairly hot oven, 400° F. (Gas Mark 6) until the pie is heated through and golden brown on top.

HUNGARIAN GOULASH

Serves 4
Cooking time: 2 hours

+ 1 *carton (¼ pint) yogurt*
+ 1 *lb. stewing steak, trimmed*
+ 2 *tablespoons paprika*
+ 2 *large onions, peeled and chopped*
+ 1 *clove garlic, crushed*
+ 3 *tablespoons tomato purée*
+ ½ *pint beef stock*
+ 1 *lb. potatoes, peeled*

Cut beef into 2 in. cubes, mix salt and pepper with paprika and roll beef in mixture, fry on all sides, remove. Prepare vegetables. Fry onion and garlic until soft, replace meat, add tomato pureé and stock, bring to boil. Stir well before adding potatoes. Cover and simmer for 2 hours, stirring occasionally. Stir in yogurt, adjust salt and pepper, reheat but do not boil.

COUNTRY BREAD BAKE

Serves 4

- ✦ 1 *pint milk*
- ✦ 8 *oz. bacon*
- ✦ 1 *oz. butter*
- ✦ 1 *onion, chopped*
- ✦ 4 *oz. mushrooms, sliced*
- ✦ 8 *slices bread, from a large white loaf*
- ✦ 3 *eggs, beaten*
- ✦ *Salt and pepper*

Divide bacon into half and chop one half. Fry chopped bacon with onions and mushrooms until soft, about 3–4 minutes. Remove crusts from bread, cut each slice into quarters. Arrange half the bread in a buttered heat-proof dish, 8 in. by 10 in., sprinkle bacon mixture evenly over bread then arrange remaining bread and the whole pieces of bacon on top. Warm milk and pour onto eggs. Beat well and season to taste. Pour over bread mixture. Cook in a slow oven, 325° F. (Gas Mark 3), for 50 minutes, until the bread is crisp and the bacon is cooked.

SCANDINAVIAN LAMB

Serves 4

- ✦ 1 (5 oz.) carton yogurt
- ✦ 1 breast of lamb, boned and cubed
- ✦ 1 tablespoon oil
- ✦ 1 medium onion, sliced
- ✦ ½ pint stock
- ✦ 1 teaspoon rosemary
- ✦ Salt and pepper
- ✦ 1 tablespoon cornflour
- ✦ 5 oz. cooked peas

Fry the lamb in oil for 15–20 minutes. Remove from the pan and drain off most of the fat. Fry the onion in the remaining fat until soft. Return the lamb to the pan and add the stock, rosemary and seasoning. Bring to the boil, cover and simmer for 1 hour. Blend the cornflour to a smooth paste with a little water and carefully stir into the lamb mixture. Bring to the boil, stirring continuously. Remove from the heat and add the sour cream and peas.

Serve with boiled rice.

TURKO-ASIAN RICE

Serves 6

- ✦ ⅓ *pint yogurt*
- ✦ *6 oz. long-grain rice*
- ✦ ¾ *pint water*
- ✦ *6 oz. onion, chopped*
- ✦ *1 clove garlic, crushed*
- ✦ *2 oz. butter*
- ✦ *1½ teaspoons salt*
- ✦ ¼ *teaspoon pepper*
- ✦ *1 teaspoon powdered ginger*
- ✦ *1 teaspoon chili powder*
- ✦ *5 oz. drained canned tomatoes*
- ✦ *3 oz. desiccated coconut*
- ✦ *3 oz. cashew nuts, chopped*

Put rice, water and salt into saucepan. Bring to boil, stir once. Cover tightly and simmer for 15 minutes. Cook onion and garlic in butter until tender. Add rice, seasonings, tomatoes, coconut and half of the nuts. Blend well. Fold in the yogurt. Heat through. Top with remaining nuts. Serve with chicken.

SECTION SIX—PART ONE
Cheese Recipes

Cheese is used throughout the world both for eating by itself and for cooking. There are literally hundreds of cheeses on the market from all over the globe—each variety with its own distinct taste.

If you're having a Wine and Cheese Party, as I like to do, you can make use of the textures and different colours of various kinds of cheeses to make the most splendid sculptures and creations—some of my favourites I'm going to outline for you later.

First, let's cook with cheese. This recipe is called Pannequets au Fondue. You might think it's a French dish by the name, but it's not—a fondue is a Swiss cheese dip, and this particular recipe is a Californian adaptation of it.

The difference is that in this dish we take the fondue a stage further, and instead of just having a cheese dip, we also make some little pancakes—pannequets—in which we put the rich fondue filling, and then cover them with sauce.

PANNEQUETS AU FONDUE PANCAKES WITH CHEESE FONDUE FILLING

Flour

Salt

Pepper

Egg

Milk

Butter

Dry white wine

Lancashire cheese

Cornflour

Kirsch

Hollandaise sauce

Cream

Crepes (makes 12):

Sift into bowl 3½ oz. plain flour and a pinch of salt. Combine 1 large egg, lightly beaten and 8 fl. oz. of milk. Strain into flour mixture and mix until batter is smooth. To cook the crepes, heat a small frying-pan from 5–6 in. in diameter until very hot. The crepes must cook quickly or they will be tough. Put ½ teaspoon butter in pan and swirl pan to coat bottom and sides. As soon as butter begins to brown pour in about 2 tablespoons of the batter and swirl pan in a circular motion to spread batter evenly and thinly to edge. Cook the crepe for about 1 minute, or until set and brown on underside, turn with spatula and cook for 20–30 seconds, or until second side browns. Turn out on greaseproof paper to cool.

Cheese Filling (fondue):

In saucepan heat 4 fl. oz. of dry white wine, but do not boil. Stir in 8 oz. crumbled Lancashire cheese and continue to stir until cheese is smooth and creamy. Stir in 2 teaspoons cornflour dissolved in 1 tablespoon Kirsch and continue to stir until the fondue simmers. Sprinkle with freshly ground pepper. Keep warm over hot water, or cool and reheat. Makes 8 fl. oz. fondue.

Hollandaise Sauce:
- ✦ *½ pint milk*
- ✦ *1 oz. flour*
- ✦ *1 oz. butter*
- ✦ *2 egg yolks*
- ✦ *3 teaspoons lemon juice*
- ✦ *Salt*
- ✦ *Pepper*

Measure flour and butter and add to milk. Stirring continually, bring to boil. Add egg yolks, lemon juice, salt and pepper. Measure 6 fl. oz. of Hollandaise sauce and fold in 2 fl. oz. of whipped cream. Preheat oven to very hot. Electric 450° F. (Gas Mark 8).

Presentation:

Spread each crepe with about 1 tablespoon of fondue. Roll up and arrange in a buttered au gratin dish large enough to hold all 12 crepes, or in individual buttered baking-dishes. Bake in a very hot oven 4–5 minutes, or until hot. Remove from oven. Spoon sauce over the crepes and put under the grill for 30–60 seconds, or until sauce is lightly browned.

In the thirteenth century cheese was used as a substitute for cement in England, when the cheese got stale, that is. I don't advocate keeping your cheese that long just to find out if it works, but it is a pretty incredible thought.

Another thing I heard when I was in Cheshire was an old custom whereby under the system of tythes in that county, the farmers used to pay their rents in cheeses. There's also a church in a little village up there which has a chest with a particularly heavy lid. Any girl who couldn't lift the lid unaided was considered unsuitable to be a cheesemaker—prospective wives were also expected to pass the test.

All good traditional cheeses have stories like that attached to them, and collecting these legends can be one of the most fascinating things about recipe-hunting.

PARTY DISHES USING TRADITIONAL CHEESES

CROCODILE CUCUMBER

+ 1 *cucumber*
+ *Few blanched almonds*
+ 4 *strips green pepper*
+ *Cubes of cheddar cheese*

Garnishes:

Cocktail cherries, olives, gherkins, coloured cocktail onions, etc.

Choose a cucumber that is suitably curved. Split broad end of cucumber lengthwise for 2–3 in. to form the mouth and prop open with a small cocktail stick. Press a few pieces of blanched almonds for the teeth. Arrange two slices of stuffed olives for eyes. Shape strips of green pepper into legs with a sharp knife and secure in place at sides of cucumber with small cocktail sticks.

MELON MONSTERS

+ 5 *oz. cream cheese*
+ 4 *oz. Derby cheese, grated*
+ 3 *tablespoons mayonnaise to thin*
+ 1 *tablespoon sherry*
+ *Paprika pepper*
+ Serve with: *Thin sticks of celery, carrot, crisps, etc.*
+ 1 *teaspoon sherry*

Mix ingredients together until of a 'dip' consistency. Any suitable ingredient may be added, e.g. fried bacon, chives, prawns. Sprinkle with paprika pepper. Serve surrounded by celery, carrot, etc.

SUNFLOWER SALAD

+ 3 *heads chicory*
+ 4 *tomatoes*
+ 2 *sticks celery*
+ 4 *oz. Leicester cheese*
+ *French dressing*

Select ten well-shaped chicory leaves, arrange on a plate. Cut two of the tomatoes into wedges. Chop remaining chicory, tomatoes and celery. Cut the cheese into cubes and add. Mix with the French dressing to bind. Pile the mixture into the middle of the plate as the sunflower 'head' with the leaves sticking out as petals. Garnish in between the leaves with tomato wedges.

BROWN BREAD HOUSE

Cut the top of the loaf so as to form the roof. Hollow out the inside of the loaf and fill with miniature sandwiches made with Cheshire cheese. 'Thatch' the roof with strips of cucumber. Use a cube of cucumber and a black olive for the chimney. Use tomato halves for edge of roof. Make windows, door, etc. Place loaf on a base, surrounded with cubes of cheese with cocktail sticks stuck in.

CHESS BOARD

+ 8 *pawns*
+ 1 *King*
+ 2 *Bishops*
+ 2 *Knights*
+ 2 *Castles*

Make the pawns with cubes of cheese, an olive and coloured cocktail onion. The castles sport a brightly coloured flag on a pin. Each side should be identical in structure but differently coloured. In 'Cooking Price-Wise', one side was made of Stilton, the other Double Gloucester.

Serve on cheese board.

PINEAPPLE AND CHEESE LOAF

+ 1 *small French loaf*
+ 2 *oz. butter*
+ 4 *oz. Lancashire cheese*
+ 8 *pineapple rings*
+ 3–4 *tablespoons double cream*
+ *Maraschino cherries*

Slit the loaf lengthwise down the middle. Spread generously with butter. Crumble the Lancashire cheese into a bowl, chop up six rings of pineapple and add. Bind together with cream and stuff the loaf. Cut remaining rings in half and decorate loaf with pineapple and cherries. Serve on an oval platter.

TOMATO BASKETS

+ 8 *large firm tomatoes*
+ 2 *oz. butter*
+ 6 *oz. Caerphilly cheese*
+ 4 *tablespoons mayonnaise*
+ *Salt and pepper*
+ *Paprika pepper*
+ *Watercress*

Cut a circle around the top of each tomato, lift off 'lid' and carefully scoop out pulp. Turn empty cases upside down to drain. Mix tomato pulp, cheese, mayonnaise, and salt and pepper together. Stuff tomatoes. Put lids back on. Garnish with paprika pepper and cress.

DECORATED TUNA FISH

Mix together one can of Tuna fish and 8 oz. grated Wensley-dale cheese, bind together with a little salad cream. Mould into fish shape on a large platter. Decorate with cucumber scales, radish fins, an olive for an eye, etc.

SUMMERTIME FLAN

Serves 4

Pastry:
+ *6 oz. flour*
+ *½ teaspoon salt*
+ *3 oz. butter*
+ *2 tablespoons water*

Filling:
+ *1 large onion*
+ *½ oz. butter*
+ *2 large tomatoes*
+ *2 eggs, hard-boiled*
+ *Salt and pepper*
+ *¼ pint double dairy cream*
+ *2 oz. Lancashire cheese (crumbled)*
+ *Watercress*

Pastry:

Sift flour and salt. Rub in butter until mixture resembles fine breadcrumbs. Add water to bind to a stiff dough. Knead lightly and leave to rest for 30 minutes in a cool place. Roll out pastry and use to line an 8-in. flan-ring on a baking tray. Fill with foil and baking beans and bake 'blind' in a hot oven, 425° F. (Gas Mark 7) for 15 minutes. Remove foil and continue baking for 7–10 minutes until golden brown.

Filling:

Slice onions and cook gently in butter for 3–4 minutes without browning. Skin tomatoes and slice. Slice hard-boiled eggs. Arrange onion in bottom of flan-case. Arrange alternate slices of tomato and hard-boiled egg on top. Season. Carefully pour over cream. Sprinkle with crumbled cheese. Replace in hot oven, 425° F. (Gas Mark 7) for 25 minutes until cheese browns.

Serve hot or cold garnished with watercress.

CREAMY DIP

- ✦ *Blend 4 oz. cream cheese with 4 oz. finely grated Derby Cheese.*
- ✦ *Thin with mayonnaise.*
- ✦ *Serve celery sticks and potato crisps to dunk in the dip.*

CHEESED PARTY EGGS

- ✦ *4 hard-boiled eggs*
- ✦ *2 oz. Derby cheese, grated*
- ✦ *3 tablespoons mayonnaise*
- ✦ *Salt and pepper*
- ✦ *Paprika*
- ✦ *8 rounds of French bread*
- ✦ *4 tomatoes*

When the eggs are quite cold, shell and halve them. Turn the egg yolks into a bowl and mash with the cheese, mayonnaise and seasoning. Spoon back into the egg-whites and sprinkle with extra paprika pepper. Serve eggs on buttered rounds of French bread, with a halved tomato.

CHEESE SPREADS

+ 2 *oz. butter*
+ *½ level teaspoon salt*
+ *½ level teaspoon made mustard*
+ 8 *oz. Cheddar cheese (grated)*
+ *Few drops Worcester sauce*
+ 3–4 *tablespoons milk*

Cream butter and add seasonings and grated cheese. Beat in the Worcester sauce and milk to make a smooth mixture. This spread will keep well for 4–5 days in a screw-top jar or plastic container, either in the fridge or in a cool place.

MORE CHEESE SPREADS

Cheese and Tomato:

+ *Mix a finely chopped onion into the spread.*
+ *Spread; top with slices of tomato.*

Cheese and Celery:

+ *Chop finely some celery and a lettuce leaf and mix into cheese mixture.*

Cheese and Anchovy:

+ *Add anchovy essence to taste to the spread. Garnish with sprigs of watercress.*

Cheese and Bacon:

+ *Crumble some crisply-cooked bacon and mix into the spread.*

Cheese and Raisins:

+ *Mix chopped raisins into the spread.*

Nuts:

+ *Mix chopped nuts into the cheese spread.*
+ *Spread these on biscuits, breads and toasts, or simply serve them in pretty pots and let your guests do their own spreading.*

CHEESE SOUFFLÉ

- ✦ *2 oz. butter*
- ✦ *2 oz. plain flour*
- ✦ *½ pint milk*
- ✦ *4 oz. grated cheese*
- ✦ *3 standard eggs (separated)*
- ✦ *2 teaspoons ready-mixed English mustard*
- ✦ *Sprinkle of salt and freshly milled pepper*

Melt butter in pan; stir in flour and cook a minute without browning. Remove from heat and stir in milk. Return to heat and cook, stirring until the mixture thickens and leaves the sides of the pan. Remove from heat and blend in the cheese. Stir in the egg yolks blended with the mustard and a sprinkle of salt and pepper. Whisk egg-whites until stiff, but not dry, and fold in. Turn into two buttered 1-pint soufflé dishes (or into three ¾-pint dishes or one 2-pint dish). Run a teaspoon round the edge of the mixture, pushing in slightly. Bake in a moderately hot oven, 400° F. (Gas Mark 6) for 25 minutes (or in three dishes for 20 minutes, in one dish for 40 minutes). The mixture should be brown outside and almost runny inside. Serve at once. Sufficient for a main course for two, a first course before main course, or savoury for four.

SHRIMP AND ASPARAGUS STUFFED PANCAKES

For the Pancake:
- ✦ *Just under ½ pint milk*
- ✦ *Pinch of salt*
- ✦ *1 tablespoon melted butter*
- ✦ *4 oz. plain flour*
- ✦ *2 eggs*

For the Filling:
- ✦ *¼ pint milk*
- ✦ *1 oz. flour*
- ✦ *1 cupful shelled shrimps or prawns*
- ✦ *About 1 lb. young asparagus*
- ✦ *1 tablespoon sherry*
- ✦ *A few mushrooms to garnish*
- ✦ *Grated cheese*
- ✦ *1 oz. butter*
- ✦ *Salt, pepper and paprika*
- ✦ *2 tablespoons parsley*
- ✦ *About 2 oz. melted butter*

Make the pancake batter by sifting together the flour and salt and mixing in the 2 eggs and most of the milk. Beat well until the surface of the batter is covered with bubbles, stir in the rest of the milk and leave to stand for at least ½ hour in a cool place. Cook the asparagus in the usual way and cut off the tips about 2 in. down the stalks. Chop the rest of the stalks. Make a sauce with the butter, flour and milk, and season well. Stir in the shrimps, chopped asparagus stalks, parsley and sherry. Make very thin pancakes by pouring about a tablespoon of batter—the amount depending on the size of the pan—into a well heated, very lightly greased heavy frying-pan. Run the batter this way and that—until it covers the bottom of the pan. Loosen edges with a palette knife and when bubbles begin to appear turn and cook on other side. As each one is made, put a share of the filling on it and roll up. Always roll pancakes with the first cooked side out. Arrange pancakes in a fireproof-dish and put in the asparagus tips so that they just protrude from them. When all the pancakes are cooked garnish with a few mushrooms and pour over the melted butter; sprinkle with grated cheese and 'glaze' in a hot oven till the pancakes are warmed through. Serve at once.

ORANGE AND LEMON CHEESECAKE

Serves 6–8

For Pastry:
- ✦ *8 oz. plain flour*
- ✦ *½ teaspoon salt*
- ✦ *4 oz. butter*
- ✦ *2 oz. caster sugar*
- ✦ *3 tablespoons water*

For Cheesecake Filling:
- ✦ *1 lb. cottage cheese, sieved*
- ✦ *1 oz. ground almonds*
- ✦ *2 eggs*
- ✦ *2 egg yolks, creamed with 4 oz. sugar*
- ✦ *Finely grated zest of 2 small lemons*
- ✦ *5 oz. carton soured cream*
- ✦ *2 oz. sultanas*
- ✦ *1 oz. finely chopped candied peel*

For Soured Cream Topping:
- ✦ *5 oz. carton soured cream*
- ✦ *1 oz. caster sugar*

To Decorate:
- ✦ *Halved slices of candied orange and lemon*

Make pastry and use to line swiss roll tin 7 in. by 11 in. by 1 in. Bake 'blind' in hot oven, 425° F. (Gas Mark 7) for 15 minutes. Mix together sieved cottage cheese, ground almonds, eggs, yolks and sugar, grated lemon zest, soured cream, sultanas and chopped candied peel. Fill pastry case with cottage cheese mixture and bake in slow oven, 300° F. (Gas Mark 2) for 1 hour 10 minutes. Spread cheesecake with soured cream and sugar mixture 15 minutes before end of baking time. Turn off oven and leave cheesecake in oven for further 1 hour. Chill. Remove from tin. Decorate with halved slices of candied orange and lemon.

POTTED CHEESE

- *¼ lb. Double Gloucester cheese (grated)*
- *2 oz. butter*
- *Pepper*
- *Pinch of ground mace*
- *½ glass dry sherry*

Pound the cheese with butter, pepper and mace. Add the sherry and mix thoroughly. Use this as a spread for water biscuits, cream crackers, cheese biscuits or small snippets of bread. Then garnish attractively with sliced olives, sprigs of parsley or a few chopped nuts.

PRAWN AND CHEESE SAVOURY

- ✦ 6 *oz. shortcrust pastry*
- ✦ *¼ pint milk*
- ✦ 2 *eggs*
- ✦ 3–4 *oz. Lancashire cheese* (*crumbled*)
- ✦ *Salt and pepper*
- ✦ 4 *oz. chopped prawns or shrimps*
- ✦ *Garnish: Parsley*

Line an 8-in. flan-ring with the pastry. Beat the milk, eggs cheese, salt and pepper together in a bowl. Add the prawns, reserving one or two for decoration. Pour the mixture into the flan-case. Bake in the centre of a moderately hot oven, 400° F. (Gas Mark 6) for 30–35 minutes until set and golden brown in colour. Decorate flan with parsley and remaining prawns. Serve hot or cold.

HAM CURL-UPS

- ✦ 8 *thin slices ham*
- ✦ 8 *asparagus tips, drained*
- ✦ 3 *oz. Caerphilly cheese*
- ✦ 4 *slices buttered bread*
- ✦ *Watercress to garnish*

Roll each slice of ham round an asparagus tip. Cut cheese into wafer-thin pieces and arrange on buttered bread. Top each with two curls of ham and asparagus, and a sprig of watercress.

ALMOND CHEESE CAKES

Cut ½ lb. Cheshire cheese into large dice. Toss these in enough meat or vegetable extract to coat them lightly—then in chopped, toasted almonds. Serve with salad.

CHEESE SHAPES

- ✦ *2 oz. butter*
- ✦ *4 oz. Leicester cheese (grated)*
- ✦ *Salt and pepper*
- ✦ *A pinch of dry mustard*
- ✦ *4 slices of toast*
- ✦ *Capers*
- ✦ *Cucumber slices*
- ✦ *Tomato and radishes to garnish*

Cream butter, add cheese, salt, pepper and mustard and mix thoroughly. Spread on the toast and cut into interesting shapes with a sharp knife or cutter. Garnish attractively with capers, tiny slices of cucumber, and pieces of tomato or radishes. The radishes should be cut crosswise several times (without severing the base) and allowed to open flower fashion in cold water.

CHICKEN LIVER RISOTTO

- ✦ 1½ oz. butter
- ✦ 1 small onion, chopped
- ✦ 4 oz. bacon, cut into 1 in. pieces
- ✦ 2 oz. chicken livers, roughly chopped
- ✦ 8 oz. uncooked long-grain rice
- ✦ 1 pint chicken stock
- ✦ Salt and pepper
- ✦ 4 oz. mushrooms
- ✦ 3 oz. grated cheese

Heat the butter, fry onion, bacon and chicken livers for 2 minutes, add the rice and cook a few minutes more. Add stock, and bring to the boil. Season and add sliced mushrooms, then cover and simmer for 20–25 minutes. Fold in half the cheese. Turn on to hot serving-dish, sprinkle with remaining cheese.

Serve at once.

HADDOCK AND MUSHROOM PIE

Serves 4

- ✦ 1 *lb. smoked haddock*
- ✦ 2 *oz. butter*
- ✦ 4 *oz. button mushrooms*
- ✦ 1 *lb. 8 oz. cooked long-grain rice*
- ✦ 1 *can (10½ oz.) condensed mushroom soup*
- ✦ *Seasoning to taste*
- ✦ 1 *oz. grated cheese*
- ✦ *Chopped parsley*

Poach smoked haddock in water until cooked (10–15 minutes). Melt the butter and sauté the button mushrooms (6–8 minutes). Flake the cooked haddock and mix into the cooked rice together with can of condensed mushroom soup, season to taste. Pour the fish and rice mixture into a casserole dish and sprinkle with grated cheese and arrange the sautéed button mushrooms on top of the pie. Place either in hot oven or under grill until brown on top. Garnish with chopped parsley.

WENSLEYDALE DIP

- ✦ *4 oz. Wensleydale cheese (crumbled)*
- ✦ *About 4 tablespoons warm real dairy cream*
- ✦ *4 chopped walnuts*
- ✦ *A little chopped watercress*
- ✦ *Pinch cayenne pepper*
- ✦ *Salt to taste*
- ✦ *Potato crisps*

Break up the cheese with a fork and work in the warm dairy cream to a fairly smooth consistency. Add the walnuts, watercress and seasoning. Serve in an attractive bowl and hand freshly crisped potato crisps with the dip.

ZEALAND CHICKENS

Serves 4

- ✦ *4 well flattened slices of veal*
- ✦ *4 streaky bacon rashers*
- ✦ *2 tablespoons chopped onion*
- ✦ *1 tablespoon chopped parsley*
- ✦ *12 oz. grated cheese*
- ✦ *4 oz. butter*
- ✦ *3 oz. plain flour*
- ✦ *¾ pint of milk*
- ✦ *Pepper*

Lay the four veal slices flat on a board. Mix together 6 oz. cheese, the chopped onion and parsley. Press into the centre of each slice of veal. Roll up each slice 'roly-poly' fashion, wrap rasher round each, tie with cotton. Fry in 1 oz. butter till golden brown. Place in shallow casserole. Make up cheese sauce using 3 oz. butter, 6 oz. cheese, flour, milk and pepper to taste. Pour over 'chickens'. Cover tightly and cook for 30 minutes at 350° F. (Gas Mark 4). Remove lid and finish for 10 minutes.

STILTON CHEESE SLAW

+ 6 *breakfast cups of shredded white cabbage*
+ 2 *tablespoons chopped green pepper*
+ 2 *tablespoons chopped green onion tops*
+ ¼ *pint sour cream*
+ 2 *tablespoons mayonnaise*
+ 1 *tablespoon lemon juice*
+ ½ *teaspoon sugar*
+ *Pinch salt*
+ 4 *oz. Stilton cheese (crumbled)*

Mix cabbage, pepper, and onion tops, and chill well. Blend sour cream, mayonnaise, lemon juice, sugar, salt and cheese, and chill. Put cabbage mixture in a bowl; pour over it the sour cream mixture.

SECTION SIX—PART TWO
Coffee

Coffee is the most abused drink that I know. It's unusual to get a really good cup in any but the most expensive restaurants, and then it's often wildly over-priced. Actually, coffee is one of the most versatile of drinks—as I hope to show you. It is also a good ingredient in many recipes.

It's interesting, I think, that coffee originally came from Ethiopia, or Abyssinia, if you prefer.

In England the coffee shop is a very old institution. In the eighteenth century there were hundreds of coffee houses in London, and it was fashionable for men to meet in a coffee house to talk business or politics over a cup of steaming hot coffee. Indeed, so much politics were talked that a proclamation banning coffee shops was issued, and for a while they were all closed.

In that time, during the closure, the art of making a good cup of coffee was lost to the British—but it is an art I now hope to revive by outlining the ancient jug method of making coffee. It is the simplest method, involves no elaborate percolators or expensive equipment, and makes the best coffee. I love coffee!

HOW TO MAKE COFFEE—
Ancient Jug Method

Allow 2 heaped tablespoons of coffee to one pint of water.

Warm the jug and add the required amount of coffee. Pour on freshly boiling water. Stir and leave to stand for a few minutes, then skim the surface with a spoon to take away the excess coffee grounds. Leave for another minute, then using a strainer, pour into cups and serve with milk or cream and sugar to taste.

CAFÉ NAPOLEON

Cognac Brandy
+ *Hot strong black coffee*
+ *Lump (or caster) sugar*
+ *Double cream*

Heat a stemmed brandy glass. Pour in one measure of Cognac brandy. Add three cubes of sugar. Fill goblet with hot strong black coffee to within 1 in. of the brim and stir to dissolve sugar. Top off to the brim with double cream poured carefully over the back of a spoon so that it floats on top of the coffee. Do not stir, as the best flavour is obtained by drinking the coffee and brandy through the cream.

CAFÉ BRULOT

Serves 6

- ✦ 6 *lumps sugar*
- ✦ 8 *whole cloves*
- ✦ 1 *in. length cinnamon stick*
- ✦ *Finely pared rind of ½ lemon*
- ✦ 6 *measures of Cognac brandy*
- ✦ 6 *small coffee cup measures hot, strong black coffee in a warmed punch-bowl*
- ✦ 6 *cinnamon sticks to stir*

Place all the ingredients except the coffee into a warmed shallow pan (or chafing dish) and ignite the contents. (Use a match, *not* a lighter for this.) Stir well until mixed. After a minute or two, slowly pour the flaming brandy into hot coffee and continue to stir. Bring the serving-bowl, still flaming, into a darkened room. As the flame subsides, ladle the contents into demitasse cups and serve. Provide cinnamon sticks to stir.

TURKISH COFFEE

Traditionally made in a special pot with white-tinned lining and a long handle called an 'Ibrik'. It can be made in a saucepan and should be served in very small or demitasse cups.

For each person pour 1 demitasse cup of cold water into the pot and bring to boil. Add 1 heaped teaspoon castor sugar per person to water. Bring back to boiling point. Add 1 heaped dessertspoon per person finely pulverized coffee. This is obtainable from specialist coffee shops. Stir well. Bring the coffee to the boil three times, removing pot from heat between boilings and tapping the base gently until froth on top subsides. After the last boiling, remove from heat and spoon some of the creamy froth into each cup before pouring coffee very slowly out of the pot. Serve iced water in glasses as an accompaniment.

ORANGE COFFEE CREAM

+ *½ pint milk*
+ *2 eggs*
+ *1 oz. caster sugar*
+ *¾ oz. gelatine*
+ *1 tin mandarin oranges*
+ *1 dessertspoon coffee essence*
+ *A few drops of vanilla essence*
+ *¼ pint double dairy cream*

Heat the milk and make a custard with the beaten eggs and castor sugar. Cook until the custard has thickened, but do not boil. Leave to cool. Dissolve the gelatine in 2 tablespoons of the mandarin orange juice, and stir into the custard. Whip up the double dairy cream until it just begins to thicken, and then fold into the custard with the coffee and vanilla essence. Pour the mixture into a wetted mould and leave to set. Turn out by standing the mould in hot water for a few seconds and decorate with the segments of orange and whipped double cream.

COFFEE WALNUT GATEAU

+ *4 oz. caster sugar*
+ *4 oz. butter*
+ *4 oz. self-raising flour*
+ *Pinch of salt*
+ *1 oz. finely chopped walnuts*
+ *1 tablespoon coffee essence*
+ *1 tablespoon milk*
+ *2 eggs*

Filling:

+ *2 tablespoons apricot jam*

Topping:

+ *½ pint double dairy cream*
+ *1 teaspoon coffee essence*

Well grease two 7-in. sandwich tins. Sieve flour and salt. Blend coffee essence and milk together. Cream butter and sugar until light and fluffy. Beat eggs, and blend into the mixture keeping it stiff. Fold in sieved flour, chopped walnuts, milk and coffee essence. Turn into two prepared tins. Bake in a moderate oven 375° F. (Gas Mark 5) for 20–25 minutes, until evenly browned, and the sandwich cakes begin to shrink away from the edge of the tins. Cool on a wire rack.

Spread one cake with apricot jam, and place over the other one. Divide the cream equally into two bowls and add coffee essence to one. Whip each bowl of cream. With a knife, lightly mark the top and the sides of the cake into four sections, and pipe rosettes of coffee cream in two opposite quarters and pipe the two remaining sections in plain double dairy cream.

CREAMY COFFEE CRUNCH

Serves 6

Pastry:
- ✦ 6 *oz. plain flour*
- ✦ 3 *oz. caster sugar*
- ✦ 1 *teaspoon salt*
- ✦ 4 *oz. walnuts, grated or finely chopped*
- ✦ 4 *oz. butter*
- ✦ 2 *egg-yolks*
- ✦ 3 *teaspoons water*

Meringue:
- ✦ 2 *egg-whites*
- ✦ 4 *oz. caster sugar*

Filling:
- ✦ 1 *oz. cornflour*
- ✦ ½ *pint milk*
- ✦ 1 *oz. caster sugar*
- ✦ 2 *tablespoons coffee essence*
- ✦ 1 *teaspoon vanilla essence*
- ✦ ¼ *pint double dairy cream (lightly whipped)*

Decoration:
- ✦ *Walnut halves*
- ✦ *Green grapes*

Pastry:

Sift flour, sugar and salt into a bowl. Add grated or very finely chopped walnuts. Rub in butter until it resembles fine bread-crumbs. Gradually add egg-yolks and water and bind together into a stiff dough. Knead very lightly. Leave to rest in a cool place for 10 minutes. Roll out pastry into a circle 9 in. in diameter. Place on a baking-sheet, prick well and bake at 375° F. (Gas Mark 5) for 25–30 minutes. Leave on baking-sheet.

FLORADORA DESSERT CAKE

Sponge:
- ✦ 3 *oz. self-raising flour*
- ✦ 1 *level tablespoon cocoa*
- ✦ 3 *eggs*
- ✦ 3 *oz. soft brown sugar*
- ✦ 1 *tablespoon coffee essence*

Filling:
- ✦ ¼ *pint double dairy cream*
- ✦ *Apricot jam*

Sieve the flour and cocoa together. Put eggs and sugar in a bowl and whisk together till thick and the mixture holds the impression of the whisk. Fold in sieved dry ingredients and coffee essence. Turn into greased 7-in. round cake-tin and bake in a moderate oven, 350° F. (Gas Mark 4) for 45 minutes. Allow to cool. Split into two and sandwich together with the whipped double dairy cream. Brush all over cake with warmed sieved apricot jam and frosting.

The Culinary Legacy
of the Price Family

In the following pages you will find treasures that showcase the culinary legacy passed down through many generations of my family.

VICTORIA PRICE
2017

The Beginning of the
Price Family Culinary Legacy

With Excerpts from
The New Dr. Price Cook Book

Over the years, people have asked me whether Vincent Price was my father's real name. Not only is the answer Yes, but he was not even the first famous Vincent Price. His grandfather, Dr. Vincent Clarence Price, was a household name in the United States in the late 1800s. As the inventor of baking powder, Price went on to hold the patents for many of the most celebrated nineteenth-century culinary products, such as extracts of vanilla and lemon, along with many other items, including some early breakfast cereals. He also wrote a number of very popular cookbooks. Dr. Price was so well known that, at the time of his death, the Chicago Tribune *dubbed him "one of the housewife's best friends."*

His youngest son, Vincent Leonard Price, went on to run one of the largest candy companies in the United States, and became head of the National Candymaker's Association. So, is it any wonder that the most famous of the three Vincents—Hollywood icon Vincent (Leonard) Price (Jr.)—would also become well known in his lifetime as a culinary expert? In a way, it was preordained. When he was born, the National Candymakers dubbed him Vincent II, The Candy Kid! He certainly went on to appreciate and share all of the sweetness of life.

It is very exciting for us to be able to share some of the recipes from this early-nineteenth-century cookbook, The New Dr. Price Cook Book. *They provide a fascinating glimpse of the long-lasting Price family culinary legacy—as well as a wonderful look at American cooking from over a century ago!*

VICTORIA PRICE
2017

174

BREADS, BISCUITS AND ROLLS

D R. PRICE'S Baking Powder may be used instead of yeast to leaven bread. It does precisely the same work; that is, raises the dough, making it porous and spongy. The great advantage of bread made by this method is in time saved, as it can be mixed and baked in less than two hours. Milk bread needs little or no shortening, and less flour is required than when water is used. Sift flour before measuring, and use level measurements for all materials.

BAKING POWDER BREAD

4 cups flour
1 teaspoon salt
1 tablespoon sugar

7 teaspoons Dr. Price's Baking Powder
1 medium-sized, cold, boiled potato
Milk (water may be used)

Sift thoroughly together flour, salt, sugar and baking powder, rub in potato; add sufficient liquid to mix rapidly and smoothly into soft dough. This will require about one pint of liquid. Turn at once into greased loaf pan, smooth top with knife dipped in melted butter, and allow to stand in warm place about 30 minutes. Bake in moderate oven about one hour. When done take from pan, moisten top slightly with cold water and allow to cool before putting away.

BOSTON BROWN BREAD

1 cup entire wheat or graham flour
1 cup corn meal
1 cup rye meal or ground rolled oats
1 teaspoon salt

5 teaspoons Dr. Price's Baking Powder
¾ cup molasses
1⅓ cups milk

Mix thoroughly dry ingredients; add molasses to milk, and add; beat thoroughly and put into greased moulds ⅔ full. Steam 3½ hours; remove covers and bake until top is dry.

CORN BREAD

1 cup corn meal
1 cup flour
4 teaspoons Dr. Price's Baking Powder
3 tablespoons sugar

1 teaspoon salt
1½ cups milk
1 egg
2 tablespoons shortening

Mix and sift dry ingredients; add milk, beaten egg, and melted shortening; beat well and pour into greased shallow pan. Bake in hot oven about 25 minutes.

SPIDER CORN BREAD

1 egg
1¾ cups milk
2 tablespoons sugar
1 cup corn meal

⅓ cup flour
1 teaspoon salt
2 teaspoons Dr. Price's Baking Powder
1 tablespoon shortening

Beat egg and add one cup milk; stir in sugar, corn meal, flour, salt and baking powder which have been sifted together; turn into frying pan in which shortening has been melted; pour on remainder of milk, but do not stir. Bake about 25 minutes in hot oven. There should be a line of creamy custard through the bread. Cut into triangles and serve.

GRAHAM BREAD

1½ cups flour
1½ cups graham flour
4 teaspoons Dr. Price's Baking Powder
1 teaspoon salt

1 tablespoon shortening
1 egg
1½ cups liquid (½ water and ½ milk)
2 tablespoons sugar or molasses

Mix flour, graham flour, baking powder and salt together; rub in shortening; beat egg and add with sugar or molasses to liquid; stir into dry mixture and beat well; add more milk if necessary to make a drop batter. Put into greased loaf pan, smooth with knife dipped in cold water. Bake about one hour in moderate oven.

NUT OR RAISIN BREAD

2½ cups flour
½ cup graham flour
¼ cup sugar
1 teaspoon salt

1 cup walnuts or raisins
4 teaspoons Dr. Price's Baking Powder
1 egg
1½ cups milk

Sift dry ingredients together. Add raisins or nuts chopped not too fine; add beaten egg to milk and add to dry ingredients to make a soft dough. Put into greased loaf pan. Allow to stand about 30 minutes. Bake in moderate oven from 45 to 60 minutes.

All measurements are level. Four level teaspoons of baking powder about equal one heaping teaspoon as heretofore used.

COFFEE RING

3 cups flour	¾ cup milk
5 tablespoons sugar	1 cup raisins, washed, drained and floured
4 teaspoons Dr. Price's Baking Powder	3 tablespoons shortening
1 teaspoon salt	1 egg
	½ cup chopped nuts

Sift dry ingredients together; add raisins; to milk add melted shortening and beaten egg; mix thoroughly and add to the dry ingredients; add more milk if necessary, to make a soft dough; roll out lightly about ½ inch thick, divide into two long strips and twist together to form a ring; put into greased pan and sprinkle with a little sugar and nuts; allow to stand about 20 minutes. Bake in moderate oven 20 to 25 minutes.

BISCUITS

2 cups flour	2 tablespoons shortening
4 teaspoons Dr. Price's Baking Powder	¾ cup milk or half milk and half water
½ teaspoon salt	

Sift together flour, baking powder and salt, add shortening and rub in very lightly; add liquid slowly to make soft dough; roll or pat out on floured board to about one-half inch in thickness handling as little as possible; cut with biscuit cutter. Bake in hot oven 15 to 20 minutes.

EMERGENCY OR DROP BISCUITS

Same as recipe for biscuits with the addition of more milk to make stiff batter. Drop by spoonfuls on greased pan and bake in hot oven 15 to 20 minutes.

WHOLE WHEAT RAISIN BISCUITS

2 cups whole wheat flour	2 teaspoons shortening
¾ teaspoon salt	1 cup milk
4 teaspoons Dr. Price's Baking Powder	4 tablespoons cut raisins

Mix well flour, salt and baking powder, or sift through coarse strainer; add shortening and rub in very lightly; add milk; mix to soft dough, add raisins. Drop with tablespoon quite far apart on greased baking tin or in greased muffin tins. Bake in moderate oven about 25 minutes.

BRAN BISCUITS

½ cup bran	3 tablespoons sugar
1½ cups flour	½ cup water
5 teaspoons Dr. Price's Baking Powder	2 tablespoons shortening
¾ teaspoon salt	

Mix thoroughly bran, flour, baking powder, salt, sugar; add sufficient water to make soft dough; add melted shortening; roll out lightly to about ¼ inch thick on floured board; cut with biscuit cutter. Bake in hot oven 12 to 15 minutes.

CHEESE BISCUITS

1½ cups flour	1 teaspoon shortening
2 teaspoons Dr. Price's Baking Powder	6 tablespoons grated cheese
¼ teaspoon salt	⅝ cup milk

Sift together flour, baking powder and salt; add shortening and cheese; rub in very lightly; add milk slowly, just enough to hold dough together. Turn out on floured board and roll about ½ inch thick; cut with small biscuit cutter. Bake in hot oven 12 to 15 minutes.

EGG BISCUITS

2 cups flour	1 egg
3 teaspoons Dr. Price's Baking Powder	2 tablespoons shortening
½ teaspoon salt	⅓ cup water
1 tablespoon sugar	

Sift together flour, baking powder, salt and sugar; add well beaten egg and melted shortening to water and add to dry ingredients to make soft dough. Roll out on floured board to about ½ inch thick; cut with biscuit cutter. Bake in moderate oven about 25 minutes.

MUFFINS, GEMS, ETC.

MUFFINS

2 cups flour	1 tablespoon sugar	2 eggs
3 teaspoons Dr. Price's Baking Powder	½ teaspoon salt	1 tablespoon shortening.
	1 cup milk	

Sift together flour, baking powder, sugar and salt; add milk, well-beaten eggs and melted shortening; mix well. Half fill greased muffin tins with batter and bake in hot oven 20 to 25 minutes.

All measurements are level. Four level teaspoons of baking powder about equal one heaping teaspoon as heretofore used.

ENGLISH MUFFINS

2 cups flour	1 teaspoon sugar
4 teaspoons Dr. Price's Baking Powder	1¼ cups milk
¾ teaspoon salt	

Sift together dry ingredients. Mix in gradually milk to make soft dough. Half fill greased muffin rings placed on hot greased griddle or shaped lightly with floured hands into flat round cakes: Bake on griddle or frying pan turning until brown and cooked through, about 15 minutes. Split and serve hot with butter.

BLUEBERRY MUFFINS

2 cups flour	¾ cup milk
3 teaspoons Dr. Price's Baking Powder	2 eggs
1 teaspoon salt	1 tablespoon shortening
1 tablespoon sugar	1 cup berries

Sift together flour, baking powder, salt and sugar; add milk slowly, well-beaten eggs and melted shortening; mix well and add berries, which have been carefully picked over and floured. Grease muffin tins; drop one spoonful into each. Bake about 30 minutes in moderate oven.

CEREAL MUFFINS

½ cup cooked hominy, oatmeal or other cereal	½ cup milk
½ teaspoon salt	1 cup flour
1½ tablespoons shortening	½ cup corn meal
1 egg	4 teaspoons Dr. Price's Baking Powder

Mix together cereal, salt, melted shortening, beaten egg and milk. Add flour and corn meal which have been sifted with baking powder; beat well. Bake in greased muffin tins or shallow pan in hot oven 25 to 30 minutes.

CORN MEAL MUFFINS

¾ cup corn meal	2 tablespoons sugar
1¼ cups flour	1 cup milk
4 teaspoons Dr. Price's Baking Powder	2 tablespoons shortening
½ teaspoon salt	1 egg

Sift together corn meal, flour, baking powder, salt and sugar; add milk, melted shortening and well-beaten egg; mix well. Half fill greased muffin tins with batter and bake about 35 minutes in hot oven.

CRUMB MUFFINS

2 cups stale bread crumbs	½ teaspoon salt
1¼ cups milk	2 eggs
1 cup flour	1 tablespoon shortening
2 teaspoons Dr. Price's Baking Powder	

Soak bread crumbs in cold milk 10 minutes; add flour, baking powder and salt which have been sifted together; add well-beaten eggs and melted shortening; mix well. Half fill greased muffin tins with batter and bake 20 to 25 minutes in hot oven.

RICE MUFFINS

1 cup flour	⅔ cup milk
2 teaspoons Dr. Price's Baking Powder	1 egg
½ teaspoon salt	1 tablespoon shortening
1 tablespoon sugar	1 cup cold boiled rice

Sift together flour, baking powder, salt and sugar; add milk slowly; then well-beaten egg and melted shortening; add rice and mix well. Half fill greased muffin tins with batter and bake 20 to 30 minutes in hot oven.

DATE MUFFINS

⅓ cup butter	2 teaspoons Dr. Price's Baking Powder	½ lb. dates
1 egg	½ teaspoon salt	
2 cups flour	¾ cup milk	

Cream butter, add beaten egg, flour in which baking powder and salt have been sifted, and milk. Stir in dates which have been pitted and cut into small pieces. Bake about 25 minutes in greased gem pans in hot oven.
For sweet muffins sift ¼ cup sugar with dry ingredients.

POPOVERS

2 cups flour	½ teaspoon salt	2 eggs	2 cups milk

Sift together flour and salt. Make a well in flour, break eggs into well, add milk and stir from center until all flour is mixed in and until smooth. Pour into hot greased gem pans and bake 25 to 35 minutes in very hot oven. If taken out of oven too soon they will fall.

All measurements are level. Four level teaspoons of baking powder about equal one heaping teaspoon as heretofore used.

Vincent's Culinary Journey Begins

With Excerpts from His 1928 Travel Journal

In 1928, seventeen-year-old Vincent Price took his first trip to Europe. He had been saving money for three years. It was his goal to see all of the great works of art and the cultural capitals of the world, about which he had been reading and studying for the last ten years of his life.

You see, my dad became an art and culture lover at the tender age of eight, when his older sister left behind a book containing illustrations of the great masterpieces of world art. He pored over that art tome every day from then on—and became determined to live a life that would allow him to spend time in the company of as much great art and culture as he could!

Having completed his junior year of high school, he embarked on a summer journey that would take him to England, France, Holland, Germany, and Italy. He kept a meticulous journal of everything he saw—a journal that the wonderful Peter Fuller has made available to everyone through his extraordinary online recreation of that Grand Tour.

In these excerpts chosen by Peter, we glimpse Vincent Price filled with the wonder that never left him—for fine art, great cities, cultural experiences, and incredible culinary and life adventures. And it is easy to see how the young Vincent Price grew up to be the Renaissance man whose mission it was to bring a work of art into every home and culinary adventure to every palate. A century has gone by, but the joy contained in these pages will never fade!

VICTORIA PRICE

2017

DATE July 22nd 1 5.28.

PLACE Holland Belgium.

Today we awoke at 5 AM to leave for Belgum + so we road to La Hague + then left for Brussells on the train. We went thru Antwerp + then to Brussells. Took a tour of the city + went out that night with Lucy + K. We were very disgusted with our hotel the Ermitage but we got on all right.

DATE July 23 . 1928

PLACE Germany .

Today we reached Köln
Cologne in the morning &
had lunch at the Kölner hof
then went shopping and then
to the Cathedral It is the most
gorgeous thing I have ever
seen. The knaves are so
beautiful that they seem like
a dream. I like Germany
more than I ever dreamed
of it is so beautiful. We
caught the train at Cologne
& went thru the Rhine Valley
to Kolbenze where we stayed
at the Reisen - Fürstenhof a
very good hotel on the Rhine
near the Moselle. Had a
swell time

DATE August 4th 1928.

PLACE Florence.

Hats Birthday sees me in Florence at 6:30. I went to the Hotel, which is very nice & then started out to shop. I bought quite a few things & there mainly the Fountain which is cute. In the afternoon I went through the Uffizi gallery & saw so many famous pictures that I was lost. The best was Madonna delleArpie by Del Sarto. Met the party at dinner & then went shopping after also.

DATE **August 2nd 1928**
PLACE **Venice**

Today was unbearably hot and they picked a walking tour around the city. Hardly anybody went. Helen, Lucy, Elizabeth & I went downtown alone. Somebody invited us to the glass factory, it was very interesting & then they took us to see how they made lace. Then we went in St Marks which is very ornate, but beautiful & saw the stone on which the transfiguration took place & another on which St John was beheaded. Saw Madonna of the Golden Foot. This afternoon we went in gondolas to the Cathedral where Titian is buried & there Canova is also. Titan's Assumption is there & Donelli's Madonna, two of the most beautiful in the world. Another moonlit evening in gondalas.

DATE **August 5th**
PLACE **Florence**

If you look anyway around you in this city you find something interesting. Today we started out to sightsee we saw the Bapistry & Giotto's tower then Dante's House (Restored) and then to the Uffizi & Pitti. Such marvelous pictures I have never seen. Then after lunch in private cars we road to Piazza Michaelangelo & then to Church of the Holy Cross where he is buried along with Michevelli. This is the Westminster Abbey of Florence. To the Hospital to see the Bambinos & then back to the Cathedral & tower saw famous bronze doors. Then we went to the Medici Chapel & saw Micheal Angelo's famous statues. We saw Cellini's Perseus & many other famous statues in the porch of the Uffizi. Including the Rape of the Sabines, a very life-like statue.

Date **August 11th**
PLACE **Rome**

Rome the eternal city the mother of Christianity the center of antiquity consumes four days well deserved.
• The Sistine chapel is very beautiful as is all the work of Michelango.
• Visited Emanuel II buried in Pantheon.

- In church of Quo Vadis there is the place where Jesus appeared to St Peter.
- St John the Lateran is one of many churches in Rome contains the heads of St Peter & St Paul & the holy table the Baptistry contains the place where Constantine stood & the singing doors.

DATE **August 12th**
PLACE **Rome**

The second days sight seeing tour.
- In St Pauls there is a glass case in which the body of St Pius V is held... on his finger is a very large diamond & his original vestments are on him... he wears a silver mask.
- In St Peters one half of the bodies of St Peter & St Paul are kept.
- Caputian church contains Guido Reni's famous Saint Michael & the decorations with skulls.
- Saw Saint Peters Church & many things Forum of Trajan where 85 cats now live. Got special permit to go thru Kings palace. St Mary the Greater has the ceiling made of solid gold brought by Columbus from his first trip to America. In the church of Saint Peter in Chains the original chains are preserved with which St Peter was bound & above Michelangelo's famous Moses. In St Pauls the other half of the bodies of the two Saints are [unreadable]. This is a new church & very beautiful in its simplicity. The mosaic of St Peter contains diamonds for his eyes.

DATE **August 20th**
PLACE **Paris & Rheims**

Today we got up at 5:16 breakfast at 5:45 leave at 6:15 to Rheims & the battle fields. We drove thru Meaux, Dormans the famous [unreadable] Woods, to the American cemetary where 4000 boys are buried then to Chateau Thierry and Rheims we saw the Cathedral & the reconstructed parts of the town. Much devastation still visible. Then onto 108 Hill where 5000 French were instantly killed, past the Hindenburg line & Back to Paris. Grave yards all along the way. Saw Richtofen's plane in a heap in an old field

DATE **August 21th**
PLACE **Paris**

Tour of the city today went to the chapel of St Louis & it was very beautiful. Then to Notre Dame which is historical as well as beautifully interesting. Saw Eiffel Tower & Trocadero. The Tomb of the unknown soldiers. After lunch we went to the Louvre where we saw Mona Lisa, Venus de Milo, Winged Victory & The Gleaners. There, too, were millions of paintings by every artists. Tonight we went to Moulin Rouge & I have seen such a beautifully costumed show. The scenery was just as gorgeous as the girls not at all risqué.

DATE **August 24th**
PLACE **Paris**

Our last whole day in Paris I spent as usual in the shops trying to get some few presents for more people. Went back to the junks shops after lunch & saw 3 small etching for which I played 6c & then some other small ones. Tonight we went to the Casino de Paris I am bound to see Paris even if it breaks me. This was a great show very clever. Then we went to Pigalle a good club where you dance on numbers & win dolls maybe. Next to the hotel to get some addresses & then we saw Paris.

We went to a place called 'Paradis' & there lay before you Paris. Smoke as thick you could hardly see, an acordian wailing some wild tunes & Nigros dancing with whites both ways. Girls try to pick you up, but you say "J'ai une femme" & then they go saying "Quelle dommage!" buts its Paris. After this we went to a place called 'Florencés' entirely run by Nigros & now all Americans & Florence her-self came & sang to us Just Bill oh Boy such dancing. That's good by Paris nightlife, Cab 6am.

The Culinary Legacy
Continues . . .
With Favorite Price Family Recipes

People often ask me: What was your favorite meal to cook with your father? I always answer breakfast. It is still my favorite meal of the day.

On Saturday mornings, when my dad was home from filming, we went into the kitchen and made breakfast together. Just the two of us. Those were always very very special times for me: I had my dad all to myself, and I knew he was sharing more than just recipes with me. He was conveying the way he moved through the world.

My dad saw himself as a big kid. He never lost his childlike sense of wonder and amazement. So to be with him was to feel that I was going to get to grow up into a world of unending learning opportunities, joy, and interests.

I knew my dad loved to cook and to eat—and I loved learning how to make the things he loved. Popovers and pancakes and scrambled eggs with bacon. But even more than that, I loved learning all his clever tips and tricks, because I felt like he was passing on things that only he knew. Little secrets that he was letting me in on. That made me feel special in a way that I don't think I will ever find the words to describe. Even now, just thinking about it fills me with a smile that blossoms from my heart out.

I loved being my daddy's girl. I always will. That is why I keep living his legacy forward.

I hope these two recipes—and the stories that go with them—will allow you to create your own special family Saturday breakfasts, to be passed on from generation to generation. Because if I have learned anything in life it is this: Living our legacies forward is a way of keeping who and what is most important alive in our hearts and in the world. Forever. In other words, when we live our legacies forward, we are extending the love that was given to us to everyone else. Because that is the only really meaningful thing any of us can ever do: Love.

These recipes are my Legacy of Love.

VICTORIA PRICE
2017

SATURDAY MORNING POPOVERS

I loved almost everything my father cooked for me as a kid (with the possible exception of ratatouille), but my ultimate favorite was his popovers. There was NOTHING better than eating a steaming hot and buttery popover right after it came out of the oven. He often served them with an extremely garlicky Caesar salad that I can still remember to this day. But they were also wonderful for breakfast, slathered with my mother's favorite bitter orange marmalade.—Victoria Price, 2017

Ingredients

+ ⅞ cup flour
+ ¼ tsp. salt
+ ¼ cup milk
+ 2 eggs
+ ½ cup water
+ 1 stick butter (melted)

Note: All wet ingredients need to be at room temperature or the popovers will not rise well.

Put the flour and salt into a large bowl. Gradually add milk, stirring all the time. When smooth, beat in eggs that you have beaten until fluffy and pale yellow. Add cup of water. Beat vigorously until batter bubbles. (You can also make this batter in a blender, on high speed for 15 seconds, with excellent results.) Preheat oven to hot (400 degrees F). Make this batter at least an hour before it is to be cooked. Beat it again just before baking. (Sounds like something out of one of my dad's movies!) In the hot oven, heat a muffin tin (six muffins). Pour about ¼ inch of melted butter in the bottom and let it get smoking hot. Pour in batter. Bake in the hot oven for 20 minutes. Then reduce temperature to 350 degrees and continue baking for 15 minutes longer.

BUCKWHEAT GRIDDLE CAKES

My dad traveled a lot when I was a child, so I treasured the rare weekends when he was home and we could make breakfast together. We had the kitchen all to ourselves, and he shared the fine art of making the perfect pancake.

Here are some of his secrets: Mix oil and butter on a skillet at a high heat. The combination of the two should prevent burning. The first pancake is usually not a keeper, so make it small and give it to your dogs. When cooking pancakes, wait until you see small bubbles all over the surface and then turn. This will ensure that the pancakes are golden brown. Serve with real maple syrup and Vincent's Scrambled Eggs: Put a healthy dollop of butter into a frying pan; then crack four eggs directly into the butter. Salt. Let the eggs start to fry, so that you see the whites forming. When this happens, use a wooden spoon to scramble the eggs directly in the pan. They will be moist with lovely flecks of bright white and bright yellow egg. Delicious!—VICTORIA PRICE, 2017

Ingredients

+ *1 cup buckwheat flour*
+ *3 tsp. baking powder*
+ *¾ tsp. salt*
+ *1¾ cups milk*
+ *2 tablespoons melted butter*
+ *2 eggs*

Add milk (buttermilk or almond milk are lovely substitutes), melted butter, and eggs well beaten to a bowl. Sift the dry ingredients together. Add the dry ingredients to the wet ingredients and beat well. Then cook as described above. Makes 8–10 medium pancakes.

Table of Equivalents

The following recipe ingredients are provided with equivalents that will be helpful when using *Cooking Price-Wise*. The amounts given below can be multiplied or divided as needed for similar ingredients not listed below.

Please note that many supermarkets and specialty stores carry a variety of products from the UK.

1 oz. **flour** = 2 tablespoons

1 **rasher bacon** = 1 slice

¾ pint **chicken stock** = 12 oz.

1 lb. **potatoes** = 3 medium potatoes

½ gill **milk or cream** = ¼ cup = 2 oz.

¼ pint **mayonnaise** = ½ cup = 4 oz.

3 oz. **grated cheese** = 6 tablespoons

½ pint **stock** = 1 cup = 8 oz.

2 oz. **breadcrumbs** = ¼ cup

1 pint = 16 oz. = 2 cups

2 oz. **mushrooms** = ¼ cup

2 oz. **butter** = ¼ cup = 4 tablespoons

8 oz. **apples** = 1 to 2 medium apples

½ pint **shrimps** = 1 cup = 8 oz.

1½ oz. **bacon fat** = 3 tablespoons

4 oz. **grated cheese** = ½ cup

1½ –2 oz. **green herbs** = approx. 2 tablespoons

Miscellaneous

cornflour = cornstarch ❖ sultanas = golden raisins

caster sugar = superfine sugar ❖ (vanilla) essence = (vanilla) extract

single cream = light cream ❖ double cream = heavy or whipping cream

plain flour = all-purpose flour ❖ digestive biscuits = graham crackers

crisps = potato chips ❖ minced beef = ground beef

vegetable marrow = zucchini ❖ aubergine = eggplant

Index to Recipes

Almond Cheese Cakes, 161
Almond & Pineapple Gammon, 72
American Ice-Box Cake, 113
American Rice Salad, 88
Apple & Citrus Soufflé, 121
Apple & Mincemeat Syllabub, 129
Apple and Orange Stuffed Bacon, 65
Apricot & Pear Rice Ring with Sauce, 116
Apricot Stuffed Shoulder, 33
Arabian Nights Pilaf, 105
Ayrshire Poacher's Roll, 58

Bacon Carbonnade, 76
Bacon Moussé, 74
Bacon Salad, 66
Baked Ham or Gammon in a Common Crust, 56
Baked Pork Chops Country Style, 35
Baking Powder Bread, 175
Beef Burgundy, 98
Beef & Cauliflower on Rice, 106
Beef Curry, 87
Beef Stroganoff with Pimento Rice, 82
Bengal Curry, 89
Bifes de Lomo Rellenos, 39
Biscuits, 176
Blueberry Muffins, 177
Boston Brown Bread, 175
Bran Biscuits, 176
Breast of Lamb with Green Herbs, 48
Brown Bread House, 148

Café Brulot, 168
Café Napoleon, 167
Carbonnade of Beef, 47

Casserole of Lamb with Cider, 46
Cereal Muffins, 177
Cheese Biscuits, 176
Cheesed Party Eggs, 152
Cheese Shapes, 161
Cheese Soufflé, 155
Cheese Spreads, 153
    Cheese & Anchovy, 154
    Cheese & Bacon, 154
    Cheese & Celery, 154
    Cheese & Nuts, 154
    Cheese & Raisins, 154
    Cheese & Tomato, 154
Chess Board, 149
Chicken Liver Risotto, 162
Chicken Solange, 100
Chicken Vermouth with Rice, 102
Chili-Con-Carne, 51
Chocolate Hazelnut Gateau, 119
Chocolate Rum, 125
Coffee—How to make it, 167
Coffee Ring, 176
Coffee Walnut Gateau, 170
Cold Sliced Forehock with Coleslaw, 70
Coq au Vin, 109
Coquilles St. Jacques, 7
Corn Bread, 175
Cornish Bacon Pasties, 64
Cornish Pasties, 24
Corn Meal Muffins, 177
Country Bread Bake, 140
Creamy Apple Crunch, 128
Creamy Coffee Crunch, 171
Creamy Dip, 152
Creamy Herring Roe Quiche, 134
Creamy Kipper Scallops, 133
Creole Potato Salad, 11
Crocodile Cucumber, 147
Croquettes, 8
Crown Pork Chops with Orange Peel, 108

Crumb Muffins, 177
Cumberland Sauce, 57
Curried Tomato Salad, 84
Cutlets Reformé, 50

Date Muffins, 177
Decorated Tuna Fish, 150
Dolmades, 30

Egg Biscuits, 176
Emergency or Drop Biscuits, 176
Empanadas Salteras, 41
English Muffins, 177

Farmhouse Chicken Casserole,
    9
Feest Y Cybydd, 7
Fillet of Beef Angus, 23
Fish Fillets Noord Zee, 5
Floradora Dessert Cake, 172
Florentine Pancakes, 118
Fried Chicken with Lemon Rice,
    104

Gammon & Vegetable Risotto, 71
Garnished Milk Chicken, 137
Gingered Collar, 71
Glazed Apricot Gammon with
    Peaches, 69
Goulash, 52
Graham Bread, 175
Greek Lemon Soup, 96
Guard of Honour, 53
Gulf Coast Salad, 78

Haddock Kedgeree, 99
Haddock & Mushroom Pie, 163
Ham Curl-Ups, 160
Hawaiian Chicken & Long-Grain
    Rice, 79
Honey Baked Bacon, 61
Hungarian Goulash, 139
Huntingdon Fidget Pie, 67

Irish Stew, 25

Lamb à l'Orange, 38
Lamb Kebabs, 54
Lamb Salad Amondine, 45
Lancashire Hotpot, 15
Liver & Bacon Paté, 75
Louisiana Strawberry Rice, 101
Lyonnaise Potatoes, 15

Mandarin Cream Crunch, 120
Manhattan Vichyssoise, 3
Matambre Arrollado, 32
Melon Monsters, 147
Milk Shakes
    Iced Strawberry Crush, 131
    Spanish Frostee, 131
    Spiced, 130
    Wimbledon Whip, 132
Minestrone, 16
Moroccan Tajine, 28
Moussaka, 49
Muffins, 176
Mulligatawny Soup, 18
Mushroom Risotto, 93

Nasi Goreng, 81
New Year Vol-au-Vent, 135
Ninos Envueltos, 34
Nut or Raisin Bread, 175

Orange Coffee Cream, 169
Orange & Lemon Cheesecake,
    158
Orange Rose Creams, 123

Pannequets au Fondue (Pancakes
    with Cheese Fondue
    Filling), 144
Pan Creole Potatoes, 13
Parmentier Soup, 10
Peppery Chicken, 94
Peruvian Peppers, 19

Pimento Rice, 82
Pineapple & Cheese Loaf, 149
Pineapple Chocolate Ring, 126
Pineapple Custard Pudding, 122
Pommes Dauphinoise, 13
Pommes de Terre Savoyarde, 2
Popovers, 177
Potato & Fish Chowder, 21
Potato Polony, 12
Potatoes with Sour Cream, 14
Potato Yahni, 17
Potted Cheese, 159
Prawn & Cheese Savoury, 160
Provençal Bacon Casserole, 62
Puchero (Boiled Beef), 36

Quiche Lorraine, 63

Raspberry Chocolate Bliss, 125
Raspberry Cream Pancakes, 124
Rhubarb Pavlova Cake, 127
Rice—Basic Methods of Cooking
    Buttered Rice, 110
    Curried Rice, 110
    Fried Rice, 110
    Golden Rice, 110
    Herb Rice, 110
    Oven Method, 110
Rice-'n'-Beef Salad, 90
Rice & Fish Portuguese, 99
Rice Muffins, 177
Rice Pear Melba, 86
Rice Salad 'Ceylon', 91
Rice-Stuffed Green Peppers, 97

Sardinian Gnocchi, 20
Saure Kartoffeln, 11
Savoury Festive Pie, 138
Scampi Provençal, 83
Scandinavian Lamb, 141
Seafood Rice Casserole, 85

Shrimp and Asparagus Stuffed
    Pancakes, 156
Shrimp Potato Bake, 25
Shrimp & Rice, 103
Shropshire Fidget Pie, 9
Sole Elegante with Fluffy Rice,
    107
Soufflé Pudding Charmian, 114
Spanish Omelette, 66
Spider Corn Bread, 175
Stilton Cheese Slaw, 165
Stuffed Loin Chops (Lamb), 48
Summer Bacon Soup, 68
Summertime Flan, 151
Sunflower Salad, 148
Sweet Potato Cake, 26
Sweetcorn & Potato Pie, 22

Tavern Bacon, 73
Terrine of Pork, 60
Tomato Baskets, 150
Tournedos Victor Hugo, 43
Turkish Coffee, 168
Turkish Yogurt Fluff, 112
Turko-Asian Rice, 142

Valencian Paella, 95
Veal à la Marsala, 92

Wellington Salad, 44
Wensleydale Dip, 164
West Country Oatcakes with
    Bacon, 73
Whole Wheat Raisin Biscuits, 176
Wilted Spinach Salad with Bacon
    Dressing, 59

Yorkshire Pease Pudding with
    Boiled Bacon, 68

Zealand Chickens, 164